# Praise for *Essaying the Past*

"Jim Cullen's new book is a tour de force – an ideal text for virtually any history course that is the least bit writing-intensive. Written with verve, insight, and a keen sense of humor, it will delight students and professors alike."—*Charles L. Ponce de Leon, California State University at Long Beach*

"Cullen's book is the ultimate insider's guide to historical writing, the new gold standard in the field."—*Kerry Walk, Director of the Princeton Writing Program, Princeton University*

"Cullen's work is a captivating, stimulating, meaningful, and insightful tool for history students (who are not always prepared to succeed in academia) and their professors (who are demanding because they want their students to succeed)."—*James Ross-Nazzal, Houston Community College*

"It's about time someone has written a lively and entertaining book on how to think and write about history. Jim Cullen's book provides an indispensable guide for students and teachers alike."—*Gregory L. Schneider, Emporia State University*

"The most inviting guide to historical research and writing I've seen: lively, colloquial, pragmatic, learned but not pedantic. Jim Cullen is the teacher we all wish we'd had. His examples range from Thucydides to Avril Lavigne, and he even offers advice on how to read blurbs."—*Steven Biel, Executive Director of the Humanities Center and Senior Lecturer on History and Literature at Harvard University, author of* American Gothic: A Life of America's Most Famous Painting

"*Essaying the Past* underscores the essential elements in essay writing and crafting the history research paper. Jim Cullen's book offers explanations and examples that are useful in critical analysis for students learning how to write like historians."—*James Barrera, South Texas College*

"There's a level of sophistication in *Essaying the Past* that is disguised by its utterly clear and engaging style. Jim Cullen tells students just what they need to know to write about the past."—*Mari Jo Buhle, Brown University*

"Clear, engaging, and eminently practical, Jim Cullen's guide to writing (and thinking) history moves to the head of the class as the best such book we have. It is truly a gift to all those who teach or learn history."
—*E. Anthony Rotundo, Phillips Academy Andover*

# Other Books by Jim Cullen

# Essaying the Past: How to Read, Write, and Think about History

## Jim Cullen

**WILEY-BLACKWELL**

A John Wiley & Sons, Ltd., Publication

This edition first published 2009
© 2009 Blackwell Publishing Ltd

Blackwell Publishing was acquired by John Wiley & Sons in February 2007. Blackwell's publishing program has been merged with Wiley's global Scientific, Technical, and Medical business to form Wiley-Blackwell.

*Registered Office*
John Wiley & Sons Ltd, The Atrium, Southern Gate, Chichester, West Sussex, PO19 8SQ, United Kingdom

*Editorial Offices*
350 Main Street, Malden, MA 02148-5020, USA
9600 Garsington Road, Oxford, OX4 2DQ, UK
The Atrium, Southern Gate, Chichester, West Sussex, PO19 8SQ, UK

For details of our global editorial offices, for customer services, and for information about how to apply for permission to reuse the copyright material in this book please see our website at www.wiley.com/wiley-blackwell.

The right of the author to be identified as the author of this work has been asserted in accordance with the Copyright, Designs and Patents Act 1988.

Wiley also publishes its books in a variety of electronic formats. Some content that appears in print may not be available in electronic books.

Designations used by companies to distinguish their products are often claimed as trademarks. All brand names and product names used in this book are trade names, service marks, trademarks or registered trademarks of their respective owners. The publisher is not associated with any product or vendor mentioned in this book. This publication is designed to provide accurate and authoritative information in regard to the subject matter covered. It is sold on the understanding that the publisher is not engaged in rendering professional services. If professional advice or other expert assistance is required, the services of a competent professional should be sought.

*Library of Congress Cataloging-in-Publication Data*

Cullen, Jim, 1962–
    Essaying the past: how to read, write, and think about history / Jim Cullen.
       p. cm.
    Includes bibliographical references and index.
    ISBN 978-1-4051-8278-2 (hbk. : alk. paper) – ISBN 978-1-4051-8279-9 (pbk. : alk. paper) 1. History–Methodology. 2. Historiography. 3. Academic writing. I. Title.
    D16.C83 2009
    907.2–dc22

                                                                2008028317

A catalogue record for this book is available from the British Library.

Set in 10/12.5pt Meridian by SPi Publisher Services, Pondicherry, India
Printed in Singapore by Ho Printers Pte Ltd

1   2009

For Nancy Sommers,
Director of the Expository Writing Program,
Harvard University,
1994–2007

# Contents

*Contents*

# Acknowledgments

It came as something of a surprise to me when I began working on this book that I've been a teacher of writing for two decades. Like a lot of people, I ended up with expertise in something I never expected and never quite actively sought. But I am lucky to have had the experiences I've had, and would like to take a moment to trace the origins of this project so that I can thank some of the people involved.

I date its beginnings to the fall of 1988, when, as required by my doctoral program in American Civilization at Brown University, I enrolled in a class in the English Department on writing instruction. Brown at the time was at the vanguard of universities that were beginning to realize that knowing something and teaching something at the college level were two very different things, and I'm grateful to have received some formal training. I'm also grateful to the still-vibrant Center for Teaching and Learning founded by (and now named for) the late Harriet Sheridan at Brown.

But the truly decisive moment in my academic career came in 1994, when, as a freshly minted Ph.D., I was hired to teach in the Expository Writing Program at Harvard by director Nancy Sommers. "Expos," as it is known, founded in 1872, was in a transitional period, evolving from a somewhat eclectic mix of scholars and writers into a more professional program with a rigorous pedagogy advanced by Nancy and her lieutenant, Gordon Harvey. These gifted teachers and administrators created a vibrant program that serves as an intellectual pillar of Harvard College (some form of expository writing is the only course required of every undergraduate). I am proud to be an alumnus, as it were, of Expos, and privileged to have worked with the gifted students who enrolled in my classes there and in the university's Committee on Degrees in History and Literature, where I taught from 1994 to 1997.

In 2001, I left Harvard to join the faculty of the Ethical Culture Fieldston School, truly one of the formative experiences of my life. Here I have had the benefit of working with a brilliant array of colleagues, including some kind enough to read parts of the manuscript. In particular, I'd like to thank Andy Meyers, my colleague in the History Department, as well as Principal John Love and Dean of Faculty Hugo Mahabir, who allowed my work to circulate. I'd also like to thank the many Fieldston students who showed up for my classes and show up in these pages.

For many years now, my academic home away from home has been Sarah Lawrence College. Undergraduates as well as graduate students there read all or parts of the book and gave me valuable feedback. Alexandra Soiseth, Assistant Director of the MFA Writing Program at Sarah Lawrence, and my wife, Professor Lyde Cullen Sizer, were instrumental in these exchanges. Thanks also to my mother-in-law, Nancy Faust Sizer, a veteran history teacher and author in her own right, who read the manuscript with sensitivity and insight.

This book was acquired for Blackwell Publishers by Peter Coveney. He first approached me with the idea years before I realized that it truly was something I wanted to do, and once I did was exceptionally generous in allowing me to stumble my way into the fold. Once there, he gave routinely gave me excellent advice with a light touch. I'm indebted as well to his former assistant Deidre Ilkson, as well as his current assistant Galen Smith, copy-editor Louise Spencely, and the production team at Wiley-Blackwell.

For reasons I don't entirely understand, my agent, Alice Martell, has graced me with kindness I will literally never be able to repay. When I wandered obliviously into legally dicey territory, she stepped in and righted my course, smoothing the way for me to complete the book with the people and in a way I hoped I could. I still can't quite believe my good fortune.

My greatest blessings are my wife and children. For many years now they have tolerated an endlessly distracted husband and father who has nevertheless always been grateful for the relief, comic and otherwise, they routinely afford him. With the passage of time I have gradually come to realize that the pleasure of their company and the collaborative dimensions of rearing children outstrip any book as sources of joy and accomplishment. They are sources of stories I will never tire of hearing.

JIM CULLEN
Hastings-on-Hudson, NY
August, 2008

# Introduction to the Student: Why Would You Look at a Book Like This?

Reading, writing, thinking: That's what your education is about. That's all your education has *ever* been about. In elementary school, it was a matter of preparing you to acquire these crucial skills. Later, you took classes in various subjects, but while the specific content may have varied – lab reports, equations, poems about the Middle Ages – it all came down to reading, writing, and thinking.

And that's what it will continue to be about even after you finish taking the last class of your academic career. A radiologist poring over a magnetic resonance image (MRI); a government accountant preparing an annual budget; a sales representative sizing up a prospective customer on a golf course: for all these people, reading, writing, and thinking are the essence of their jobs (even if what they're reading, writing, or thinking about happens to be numbers or faces rather than words). At any given moment one of these skills may matter more than the other, and any given person may be better at one than the others. But every educated person in modern society is going to have to be able to do all three. Indeed, that's precisely what it *means* to be educated in modern society. The faster and more gracefully you do these things in your chosen field, the more likely you are to reap the rewards it has to offer – and in some fields, the rewards are impressive indeed.

History, the subject of this book, is not one of those fields. Very few people get rich doing it. Certainly, lots of people, myself among them, have been seduced by its charms. For some, it's a vocation, a lifelong commitment. For others, it's an avocation – not a livelihood, but treasured for that very reason, a source of pleasure affording relaxation and wisdom in an otherwise crowded and stressful life. Of the seemingly inexhaustible list of things human being do for fun – passions other human beings regard as curious, if not downright bizarre – history is a single star in a crowded night sky.

Writing essays, the vehicle through which this book explores the subject of history, has a lot less intrinsic appeal. No one gets rich writing essays (on just about any subject – the most commonly read variety are those published on the op-ed pages of newspapers). And almost no one regards producing an essay as a relaxing experience, though there are people, admittedly not many, who do enjoy reading them. Under such circumstances, you may well wonder why so many teachers in so many schools ask you to produce them over and over again in more courses than you can count. It would be easy and understandable to conclude that the practice is at best a matter of marginal relevance, and at worst a waste of your time.

Understandable, but wrong. Actually, there are few better pedagogical tools for an educator than a well-conceived essay assignment. The chief reason for that is the chief premise of this book: there is no better way to simultaneously intensify and fuse the experiences of reading, writing, and thinking than producing an essay. As I hope the ensuing pages will show, to really write well, you need to read well (and history, so rooted in sources, makes a special demand for reading). To do both, you really need to think hard – a habit, like physical exercise, that is both demanding and rewarding. Conversely, the experience of *having* read and written strengthens thinking, specifically a kind of thinking so central to the life of the mind: analysis.

Analysis is the keystone of this intellectual arch (and the topic of the keystone chapter of this book). It bridges reading, writing, and thinking, and is in effect the essence of what we typically call intelligence. It is a tremendous human achievement that takes manifold forms. Analytic talent is difficult to attain – and maddeningly difficult to teach. Despite countless attempts to quantify, mass-produce, and distribute a fast and cheap methodology, coaxing analysis out of students remains a highly labor-intensive skill for student and teacher alike. In the humanities, at least, we have yet to find a better tool for seeding fine minds than the traditional college essay.

Teachers may plant the seeds, but it is students who stretch and grow. It is important in this regard to recall that the word "essay" is not only a noun, but a verb: to *essay* means to try, attempt, test. The best essays have a wonderfully provisional quality, a sense of discovery as propositions are entertained by reader and writer alike. The experience can be difficult and exhausting for both, and yet there are also moments of breaking free, when suddenly a sense of flow is achieved and a genuine joy in learning takes place. That's when all the hard work seems worth it. I suspect that if you're reading this book you've had that experience at some point in your life. It's my sincere wish that you will have it again repeatedly, and that this slim book will aid you in that enterprise.

If it does, I don't assume it will be because you read it straight through from beginning to end. Certainly, you can read it that way; I wrote it in the hope that you would. But I also strived to create multiple entry points, whether in individual chapters, or in the appendices, and point out places where you can jump for more information on particular points. That said, I think of this as less of a manual than a suggestive meditation. My model was novelist and essayist Anne Lamott's arresting little 1994 book *Bird by Bird: Some Instructions on Writing and Life*. Lamott addresses fiction writers, something I decidedly am not. But she is nevertheless fascinating in her discussion of her craft, and while I would never claim this book is remotely as entertaining as that one, I was nevertheless inspired by her work to try my hand at writing a book about the craft of history.

That said, I am not going to make a special claim for my adopted discipline in this Introduction. I have the rest of the book to do that, and my goals here are to make a broader pedagogic statement about the role of reading, writing, and thinking generally. I will say, however, that I define history in a broad and humanistic way. Not having been formally trained as a historian – my doctorate is in American Studies – I lack expertise in some methodologies, particularly quantitative ones, that many scholars might well regard as crucial, if not indispensable. If nothing else, I bring a convert's enthusiasm to the subject. My best hope for evangelizing lies in the power of my examples, of showing rather than telling. I hope you'll see that as helpful.

# Part I
# Reading to Get Writing

# Chapter 1
# It's About Time

- Living with the past
- Good history gives you hope
- A habit in time

So here you are, facing the prospect of writing some history.

I don't imagine it's an especially comfortable feeling – if it was, you probably wouldn't be reading this book. I am, in any case, here to reassure you: this won't be so bad. Actually, by the time you get your diploma, you have a reasonably good chance of feeling pretty good about your history with History.

I realize that this is not something you regard as a given. That's not to say you find history to be a boring subject; you may have even chosen with enthusiasm the course you're currently taking. But you're not a professional, and if you don't find the practices of working historians daunting, you might find them mysterious or even annoying. So however you may be feeling at the moment, it's worth posing a question at the outset: Why are you doing this?

The obvious answer, of course, is that someone told you to – a parent, an advisor, or, most directly, the teacher who dispenses your assignments and your grades. You didn't make the rules of the academic game; you're only trying to play by them as honestly as you can. But if that's as far as this goes – you're doing your homework simply because you've been assigned it, no questions asked – then you've got a problem. If you're not a little curious, restless, or even little annoyed about *why* you're doing it, then you're not paying attention. And you're not getting educated.

## Living with the Past

Consider all those history teachers you've had: Why do *they* do it? They no longer need good grades. Chances are it's because they've got mortgages or other bills to pay. But that's almost surely not the original reason they got into this business – there are lots of ways to make money. At some point in their lives, they decided history was fun. Maybe that's still true.

At least initially, it wasn't an active decision. Maybe one of your teachers' mothers got her some books out of the library when she was seven years old that she liked. Or maybe the uncle of another took him to a museum. Or the teacher of another one of your teachers praised her as a kid in a way she found surprising and pleasing. And so she acquired the habit, the way some people get in the habit of playing golf or protecting the environment. Eventually, these people found themselves making a living off that habit, a living that almost certainly includes some writing, along with a lot of reading.

Maybe that idea appeals to you, maybe not. One thing's for sure: If history is nothing more than a paycheck, it's going to be lifeless. Whoever you are, the payoff is going to have to be more satisfying than that if you're going to stay with it.

Plenty of people have decided that History isn't, in fact, worth the trouble. "History is bunk," Henry Ford once reputedly said. Actually, what he really seems to have said, in a 1916 interview with the *Chicago Tribune*, is that "History is more or less bunk. We don't want tradition. We want to live in the present, and the only history that's worth a tinker's damn is the history we make today."[1] (Ford's attitude lives on in contemporary lingo, where the phrase "that's history" is meant to connote the irrelevance of the topic in question, like a relationship you consider convenient

---

[1] For the background and some analysis of this famous quote, see Robert Lacey, *Ford: The Men and the Machine* (Boston: Little, Brown, 1986), 238–9.

to forget.) Yet the man whose cars and the assembly line he perfected symbolized modernity a century ago was obsessed by the past. In the 1920s, he built an entire town, Greenfield Village, as a museum of American life as he remembered it from his childhood. It was a pretty good re-creation, and remains a model for living history museums. Nevertheless, Ford's memory was somewhat selective: It had no bank, no lawyer's offices, and no bars.[2] Facts, it's clear, don't always get in the way of history.

When history isn't irrelevant, it can be a crushing burden. "History," says Stephen Daedalus, a character from James Joyce's famous 1922 novel *Ulysses*, "is a nightmare from which I'm trying to awake."[3] In the classic socialist anthem "The Internationale," tradition is a something to be overthrown in the quest to usher in a better world. Maybe Henry Ford was right: Some things – most things? – are better off forgotten.

Indeed, you really do have to wonder whether learning about the past can make all that much of a positive difference in a person's life. Sure, it might be useful to be aware, for example, that you have a family history of alcoholism. But you don't need a three-credit class for that. Really: Is learning *anything* about, say, the Ming Dynasty likely to make a difference in your future career? For a while, I would open my U.S. history courses by asking my students about why, other than some tedious distribution requirements, anyone should bother. Invariably, I heard variations on George Santayana's famous dictum, echoing Euripides and Thucydides, that "those who cannot remember the past are condemned to repeat it."[4] All right, then, I would tell the students

---

[2]  Lacey, 248.

[3]  James Joyce, *Ulysses*, the corrected text (1922; New York: Random House, 1986), 28.

[4]  In *Phrixus*, a play that now only exists in fragments, Euripides writes, "Whoso neglects learning in his youth/Loses the past and is dead for the future." In the first book of his history the Peloponnesian War, Thucydides expresses the hope that his work "will be judged useful by those inquirers who desire an exact knowledge of the past as an aid to the interpretation of the future, which in the course of human things must resemble if it does not reflect it." My source for all three quotes (and translations) is *Bartlett's Familiar Quotations*, 16th edn., ed. by Justin Kaplan (Boston: Little, Brown, 1992), 69, 71, 588.

wryly, you'll know better than to start a land war in Asia. But of course, virtually nobody is ever in position to start a land war in Asia. Nor, for that matter, is virtually anybody in a position to stop one once one starts.

I should add that large numbers of people may collectively stop a war they find problematic or wrong, and that a sense of history can shape the perceptions that make opposition possible. But the "lessons" of the past are nothing if not slippery. The classic example is the so-called Munich analogy, wherein American policymakers wished to avoid the mistakes of European leaders in appeasing German Chancellor Adolf Hitler, as British Prime Minister Neville Chamberlain did at a 1938 meeting, leading to the Second World War. But the moral they drew from this story, that their opponents (in this case, Communists) must be resisted at all costs, led to quagmires in Korea in the 1950s and Vietnam in the 1960s. By the 1970s it had become common sense that Americans should never start a land war in Asia, proverbial wisdom which policymakers ignored by going to war with Iraq in 1991 and again in 2003 – two wars with very different results. So much for the predictive power of analogies.

## Good History Gives You Hope

So: History is irrelevant, history is depressing, history is maddeningly ambiguous. But what may be worst of all is that history is boring. Or, more accurately, History – the professional kind, with teachers and classrooms and assigned reading – is, shall we say, less than incredibly exciting. Movies like *Gladiator* and *Saving Private Ryan* are okay, but history books are often deadly. Actually, the act of reading *itself* is often deadly. So what's the point? *Why* is history worth your time? Why *should* it seep into your consciousness?

One answer is hope. Good history gives you hope.

This may strike you as a thin, vague, even foolish, assertion. Actually, some of us look upon hope with suspicion. Hope means potential disappointment. It means failure that's all the more acute when there's a belief that things could have been otherwise.

Hope is risky. It may lead you to commit to things that could hurt you – and it's painful even before the outcome of whatever it is you're hopeful about, because it often leads to stress and anxious uncertainty. In many respects, life would be easier without hope.

But even if we grant the desirability and utility of hope, you still have to wonder if *history* is really the best source of it. Remember that James Joyce line, history as "a nightmare from which I'm trying to awake." Of course, if you're an Irishman in the early twentieth century, history, particularly that of Ireland in the preceding 350 years or so before Joyce wrote his promethean novel, was for many a particularly dreadful nightmare. American history isn't so bad – unless, perhaps, you're an African American born before, say, 1950, or a Chinese immigrant born, say, after 1850, or someone with a family history of alcoholism. And yet there have been lots of people and movements in American history, from the Puritan migration of the early seventeenth century to the Civil Rights Movement of the mid-twentieth, that have not only made life better for people of the time, but have also given justified hope to succeeding generations that they too can wage and win comparable struggles. Even Ireland is now a sunnier place for many of its people than it has been for centuries. Then again, intolerance, poverty, and racism have not exactly disappeared, either. It sort of depends on how you look at it – and explaining just how you *do* look at it, whatever *it* happens to be, is one of the things good history does.

One of the things history also does is allow you to live a more vibrant life in the present. I was 41 years old when Kanye West released "Jesus Walks," the hit song from his 2004 album *The College Dropout*. I'm the wrong demographic for hip-hop – a (late) Baby-Boomer, a child of rock and roll. But I immediately recognized a number of things going on in that song. In the most immediate sense, it's a commentary on the time of its release – a time of war, terrorism, urban strife, and social division about the role of religion in public life. But it also resonated in a series of concentric circles that included the history of hip-hop (West as a middle-class revisionist to the gansta rap that dominated the turn of the century charts); the gospel tradition and its place in

11

African American music (West sampled a song by the Arc Choir, whose name is an acronym for the Addicts Recovery Center in Harlem); and the role of the Bible in everyday life (West cites the 23rd Psalm in the song). A sense of history has allowed me to understand and experience life outside my immediate background, to enlarge my sense of experience.

Let's say you're willing to grant that history is helpful, history is hopeful, and history is fun. Does it follow that you would actually want to produce any yourself? The difference between reading history and writing it is like the difference between watching a ballgame from the stands and actually playing on the field. The former has its pleasures, for sure. But the latter is literally where the action is, even if you're not a pro.

Of course, writing history isn't easy – as with playing ball, you can work up quite a sweat. Actually, writing just about anything longer than a shopping list isn't easy – it's about the most intellectually complex thing you typically undertake in your life. Inexperienced writers sometimes think struggling with an essay is a sign that something is wrong, that they have a defective intelligence, that other people play on laptop keyboards as if they're concert pianists. But if you find writing hard, all I can say is: Welcome to the club.

## A Habit in Time

One of the core characteristics of people like historians is that they master habits of thought – *analytic* habits of thought – that have real utility in everyday life. (For more on what I mean by the term "analytic," see chapter 7). These habits help one sort out the various and conflicting messages one gets continuously, from advertisements on television to criticism by a loved one, and assess their significance and credibility. They help one figure out what one really thinks – and feels – when confused, even irritated, by such messages. And they help one persuade someone else to think similarly. This emphasis on fostering analytic skills lies at the heart of this book. There's no better way of doing that than writing.

Of course, fostering analytic skills is the hallmark of any number of disciplines. What history has to offer is not simply knowledge of the past, or an awareness of recurring themes in people and societies, but rather a kind of lens – specifically a consciousness of time – which can heighten and intensify one's experience and desire to express oneself.

People sometimes convey a sense of admiration for a person, place, or thing that they consider "timeless." They're suggesting that the subject in question never goes out of style, seeming to transcend change. What I'm talking about here, however, is closer to what may be termed "time*ful*," an understanding that such people, places, and things are intriguing not because they escape history but rather because they are thoroughly saturated in it. Like a sense of place is for an anthropologist. Or a sense of character is for a dramatist. Time isn't the only lens through which to look at the world. It may not be the best lens in any given situation. But it's one that adds a real dimension to life and is worth taking seriously when you're listening to Kanye West – or exploring the history of slavery and its legacy in American life.

Of course, to really understand how a song like "Jesus Walks" ever came to be, you need to know something about hip-hop – its language, its traditions, its best-known practitioners. You surely know people who are experts in the field. They've immersed themselves in this world, and take understandable pride in their mastery of arcane detail as well as their ability to explain what what's going on the first time they hear a song. Becoming a historian is not that different: Here too there's a lingo, a set of conventions, some inside knowledge. You don't have to know all of it to be admitted to the party. But knowing a little might help. So come on in, and I'll show you the layout of the room and some of the major players. Then I'll show you a few tricks of the trade to allow you to work the floor on your own.

# Chapter 2
# What's the Story with History?

- Disciplinary measures: a profession takes shape
- Plural pasts

In the beginning, it was about stories, as the very word "history" suggests. (Actually, its roots are in the Greek word for "inquiry.")[1] The key is that it was written down, whether on clay, scrolls, or papyrus – the stories may have been oral, but we only know about them because they were recorded at some point along the way. Many ancient peoples kept little or no such records, and thus have no recoverable history in this sense (though archeologists and others can reconstruct their pasts through other means). Among the exceptions were the Jews of ancient Israel – the so-called "people of the book." Compared to their peers, they were downright obsessive about documenting their past, though their imperatives were more religious than historical.

In an important sense, History began with the Greeks. Like the Israelites, they recorded stories for religious reasons or to celebrate their sense of themselves as a people, as in the case of the great epic poems, *The Iliad* and *The Odyssey*, which date from approximately the eighth century BCE. But with the work of Herodotus (484 BCE–ca. 425 BCE) in the fifth century, we begin

[1] *The American Heritage Dictionary of the English Language*, 4th edn. (Boston: Houghton Mifflin, 2000), 833.

to see some of the recognizable aspects of history as we have come to know it, in particular an effort to confirm and report facts, provide logical causation, and render more than one side of a story. These techniques were consolidated and extended a generation later by Thucydides (ca. 460 BCE–395 BCE), whose *History of the Peloponnesian* War (written during the conflict of 431–404 BCE, in which he fought) was notable for the way it did not use supernatural explanations for events. As in so many other ways, the Romans modeled their history on the Greeks, though many histories of the Roman republic and empire – among them the biographies of Plutarch (46–127 CE), himself Greek – had a more explicitly moral tone than earlier Greek histories did.

The tendency to impart overt lessons remained a durable characteristic of historical accounts long after the fall of the empire. For much of the next thousand years, history was a handmaiden for religion and politics, a tool used to justify the status quo – or the ambitions of those who would overthrow it. Facts were secondary to the morality of the writer (or, more to the point, his patron). This pattern remained in place into the early modern era, as wars over religion gave new urgency to the use of history to justify sectarian politics and sectarian violence.

By the eighteenth century, historians affected by the intellectual currents surrounding the Enlightenment tried to correct these excesses. They placed new primacy on accuracy and objectivity. This emphasis on dispassionate analysis was the hallmark, for example, of Edward Gibbon's *The History of the Decline and Fall of the Roman Empire*, published in six volumes between 1776 and 1789. Yet this approach was not without its critics. Perhaps the most important (though not as much in his own time as later) was the Italian writer Giambattista Vico. In his much celebrated *Scienza Nuova* (*The New Science*, 1725) and other works, Vico emphasized that mere facts alone could never fully capture the truth of the past, that imaginative reconstruction and a desire to understand people on their own terms must also be a part of the equation. The debate over how objective or rational knowledge of the past can ever be has been perhaps the single most enduring conversation in history over the course of the last three hundred years, a kind of pendulum that continues to sway in our own time.

## Disciplinary Measures: A Profession Takes Shape

For our purposes, though, History became recognizably modern in the nineteenth century. Until then, it had been largely a genteel craft practiced by gentlemen of leisure, people with the resources to travel, reflect, and acquire source material on their own. Two interrelated things happened to create a new class of professionals who made a living by writing and teaching (not usually in that order). The first was the development of the modern university system that included graduate schools, the awarding of doctorates, and a system of peer-reviewed research. History was reborn as a *discipline* – a series of protocols to be learned, taught, and reproduced in an educational setting. This happened first in Germany under the leadership of the empirically minded historian Leopold von Ranke, and spread rapidly to the rest of Europe and the United States.

The second major development is that history fell under the sway of the new social sciences – and, arguably, became one itself. In the second half of the nineteenth century, a series of major contributions to human knowledge led by the publication of Charles Darwin's *Origin of Species* in 1859, coupled with technological innovations in transportation and communication, accelerated the growing prestige of science in Western intellectual life. Emerging fields like sociology and psychology explicitly patterned themselves on scientific practices and logic; older ones like philosophy and history reoriented themselves around a language of measurement, evidence, and hypothesis. Long gone were the days when a learned man like Benjamin Franklin could read widely and feel equally at home in literature as well as science. Now true knowledge and insight were understood to be tightly framed and empirical. The case study replaced the panoramic canvas. Academic history was now not typically a sweeping narrative, but a series of discrete bricks that would someday constitute a tower of truth. Such bricks, known as monographs, became staples of the profession.[2] Not all historians bought into this new paradigm as the twentieth century began. Some (particularly the old-timers who continued to work outside the new academic system) stubbornly insisted that history was an art, not a science, no less now than it had been for the ancient Greeks, for whom History was one of the nine muses. Many historians remained skeptical that one could ever achieve the kind of objective description of reality to which science aspired – human beings could not be isolated and tested in laboratories. Moreover, many of the "facts" they insisted were "objectively" true – like the racial superiority of Caucasians – looked suspiciously like self-interest masquerading as science. The critics of these skeptics, in turn, pointed out that they ran their own risks. If "reality" is in the eye of the beholder, who was to say that the anti-Semitic version of German history peddled by Adolf Hitler and his Nazi apologists was any less true than that of his democratic opponents?[3]

This history is worth bringing up because we very much live with it today – and you will very much have to contend with it every time you write History. You will be judged to a great extent on the degree to which your work accords with academic norms established in the nineteenth century – criteria like the quality of your data, your ability to respond to skeptics who offer alternative explanations for your findings, and your skill in documenting previously unknown phenomena. On the other hand, you'll quickly learn that there are no obvious formulas in History, and that a sense of personality, even character, is impossible to escape (or relinquish). And you will have to navigate between your values

---

[2]  Much of this summary of the emergence of the modern university and the place of history in it derives from Dorothy Ross, *The Origins of American Social Science* (New York: Cambridge University Press, 1991).

[3]  The classic discussion of this controversy is Peter Novick, *That Noble Dream: The "Objectivity Question" and the American Historical Profession* (New York: Cambridge University Press, 1988).

and things you know to be true and dealing with people – readers – who may not necessarily accept what you take for granted.

## Plural Pasts

There's one other thing you're going to have to contend with, too, something that is also a byproduct of this seminal moment in the history of History: the sheer profusion of variety in the discipline. Once upon a time, History was a matter of chronicling battles and leaders, of Great Men and their minions. The primary sources for such accounts were government documents and the testimony of those who had lived the events in question. Over the course of the twentieth century, this version of History became less dominant. In 1929, French historians Marc Bloch and Lucien Febvre founded an influential journal, *Annales d'histoire economique et sociale* (*Annals of Social and Economic History*) whose associates and sympathizers came to be known as the "Annales School." These historians moved away from traditional accounts of change over time among the leaders of nation states and instead focused on everyday life and its continuities – the so-called *longue duree* (long term).

In the United States, the sensibility of the Annales School was most decisively carried forward by the New Social History that emerged in the 1970s, much of it inspired by the Civil Rights and antiwar movements of the sixties. These historians sought to bring an avowedly democratic character to the discipline, to write history "from the bottom up." Whereas earlier generations of historians had wondered if there was even enough source material to know what happened during slavery, for example, these writers were able to unearth and reconstruct the world the slaves made. They made similar strides for women, working people, and other historically marginalized groups. The paradox of this movement, however, is that the New Social History seemed increasingly arcane and irrelevant to the very people it was written about (and, ideally, for). Moreover, the sense of narrative cohesion, of storytelling, once so central to conceptions of history, was increasingly lost.

Fortunately, this was not the only thing going on. Intellectual history – the notion that great ideas might matter at least as much as great men – had elbowed its way into the discussion early on. By the 1980s, cultural history – the notion that ordinary (and some extraordinary) ideas of ordinary people might matter too – had established a strong presence in colleges and universities. So did a number of other subdisciplines, among them environmental history, gender history, and memory (the shifting way events in a society are recollected and reconfigured). In the 1990s, some historians fell under the sway of postmodern literary critics who emphasized the way relations of power shaped our notion of knowledge, while some literary critics fell under the sway of historians who emphasized the importance of historical context in understanding the meaning of literary documents. Amid the ebb and flow of such currents, older kinds of history continued to flourish (indeed, traditional military history, for example, was revitalized by the influence of social and cultural history).

Now: Why should any of this matter to you? For two reasons. The first is that you have come of age at a time of great historical pluralism – your options are virtually limitless, though the sheer variety and quantity of history may seem daunting. The other is that this little overview is meant to foreground the concept of *historiography*, i.e. the history of history as a discipline. Any topic in the field that you study is going to be subject to multiple opinions, and you'll quickly find that many of those opinions are a function of the time in which they're produced. Sometimes even *disagreements* among historians are a function of a time when they're produced; the things people might fight fiercely over in one generation come to be regarded as settled, if not trivial, in the next. As you get experience in eavesdropping on historical conversations, you'll get better at sensing ideological agendas and disciplinary affinities. Just remember: Nothing in history quite speaks for itself. You have to listen hard and look broadly to really get a sense of what's going on.

Are you a little worried? Good – a *little* worried is optimal. The past keeps changing, but it doesn't necessarily change that much. Staying alert is the key. Let's wade in a little deeper and begin to really grapple with how you're going to do history yourself.

# Chapter 3
# The Sources of History

- Primary and secondary sources
- Obscure references, Maine events
- Scarcity and plenty

How do we know what we know?

The most immediate means, of course, is our own bodies: We see the clouds, we feel the heat and humidity, we may even smell impending rain. Of course, our senses are not infallible (it may not be as hot as we think), and we're not always paying attention (so absorbed in watching a ball game that we don't hear a rumble in the distance). But for most of us, the most reliable knowledge is that which we experience first-hand, the very metaphor indicative of a sensory encounter.

But to a great – and, perhaps, surprising – extent, most of what we know comes from other people. We may actually go to the ballgame, and thus witness events that may have affected the outcome (like, say, an argument between the pitcher and catcher that leads to a wild pitch). But we're likely see and hear things we previously missed, or see familiar moments from a different angle, when we watch instant replays on the evening news, read about the game in the sports section of the newspaper the next morning, or listen to a self-appointed expert at the bar as he holds forth over a beer on Saturday night. All contribute to what we "know" about the game. Only when we pause to consider *how* we know what we do, and actively *weigh* the validity of one account against another, are we likely to realize how dependent we are on information from others.

This dependency is something professionals of many kinds understand very well, however. Journalists, for example, talk to lots of people in fashioning an account of events that range from ballgames to deadly fires. Lawyers depose witnesses in the attempt to reconstruct the moment when a crime was committed or a marriage unraveled. Both are highly aware that there are different *versions* of the same event, and depending on their own perspectives (or who's paying their salaries) will favor one account over another in their reconstructions of reality for commuters on a train or jurors at a trial.

Historians are also in the business of reconstructing reality, and they too consider their own perspectives and who's paying their salaries (though this is sometimes a more subtle matter for them than it is for lawyers). But there's an important difference between the kind of work they typically do and that of journalists and lawyers – or, for that matter, scientists reconstructing natural conditions in laboratories. That difference is *time*. The accounts historians rely on are not usually first-hand; most often they're written down in limited or even fragmented ways, typically by people who are long since dead. The line between what historians and other professionals do is not absolute, of course. Sometimes a journalist will do historical research in the attempt to put a contemporary event in context, and sometimes a lawyer will use the words of dead people in constructing a narrative for listeners. And every so often, a historian will be able to discuss (or, rarely, experience) an event with its principals, the way a journalist will. But in general, it is the element of time that distinguishes the work of a historian from that of other people who write.

More specifically, historical writing is decisively shaped by the way time creates a relative scarcity of information. For journalists, it is typically time itself that's scarce – there are lots of potential people with whom to talk, but a looming deadline that sets priorities about who's going to get the most attention, which may involve persuading someone with information to admit they have it. Historians, by contrast, are relatively insulated from deadlines, which when present are measured in years rather than hours. But they often have a lot less to work with. This may seem counter-intuitive to you: It's hard not to enter a library or a bookstore and not seem overwhelmed by the sheer volume of volumes that groan on the shelves (this of course assumes you're not simply typing words into a search engine and getting thousands of hits, which can be no less overwhelming). Yet it is the quest to find information – in particular *new* information, even if it's only nuggets that will rearrange the facts of a familiar story – that goes to the heart of the contemporary historical enterprise.

Put two historians in a room to discuss their work and within minutes one will ask the other, "So what are your sources?". *Sources* are the very tissue of historical scholarship, what instruments are to musicians, or what ingredients are to chefs – you simply can't do without them. Journalists need sources too, but, again, theirs tend to be those in the realm of *now*, not *then*, and they're more likely to be people they meet at a bar than documents they discover at an archive. Journalists, you might say, rake; historians dig. (So do novelists, who often need sources too, some historical, to invent imaginary times, places, and people.)

## Primary and Secondary Sources

Historians typically distinguish between two kinds of sources. The first, and most important, are *primary* sources. You might liken a primary source to what a lawyer would call a witness, a first-hand account. That's largely true, but not precisely so. Again, the issue is time: a lawyer thinks of a witness in terms of place (was the person there?), whereas a historian thinks in terms of time (was the person there *then*?). A diary entry by someone who observed a murder is certainly something a historian would consider a primary source. But so is a newspaper account published the next day. Depending on the circumstances, a historian might prefer one to the other, but they're both usually considered primary sources.

*Secondary* sources, by contrast, are subsequent accounts of an event, recorded at some distance (ranging from years to centuries) afterward. The great disadvantage of secondary sources is that they lack immediacy. You've heard the phrase, "you had to be there," used to explain the truism that mere facts can't quite capture the experience of an event. Secondary sources never are "there." The great advantage they typically have, however, derives from this very fact – they put an event in context, often using multiple primary sources that make it easier to understand and its significance easier to appreciate. Indeed, secondary sources make it possible for people who come upon them later to know an event better, i.e. to see its long-term consequences, in the way those who rely solely on primary sources never can. In effect, they can create a kind of illusion of being at two places (like, say, in opposing dugouts during a legendary game) at the same time.

The line between a primary source and a secondary source is not always hard and clear. Sometimes, particularly in the realm of ancient history, a document recorded within a century of an event or a life will be considered virtually primary. There are also times that secondary sources are treated as primary sources. In my first book, *The Civil War in Popular Culture*, I analyzed poet Carl Sandburg's famous multivolume biography of Abraham Lincoln not as a document of Lincoln's life so much as Sandburg's, and not so much as a biography that told readers about the Civil War, but rather as one that revealed, intentionally and not, a good deal about the years between World War I and World War II, when Sandburg wrote it.[1] This kind of work goes on all the time, particularly among cultural historians.

Some historians also make a distinction between secondary sources and *tertiary* sources, which are the most general works of history, like encyclopedia articles or textbooks, which rely more on secondary sources than primary sources. Tertiary sources are often a terrific way to begin research on a subject (something I'll have more to say about in the next chapter), but are not usually

---

[1]  Carl Sandburg, *Abraham Lincoln: The Prairie Years*, 2 vols. (New York: Harcourt, Brace, 1926); *Abraham Lincoln: The War Years*, 4 vols. (New York: Harcourt: Brace, 1939); for my treatment of Sandburg's biography as a primary source, see Jim Cullen, *The Civil War in Popular Culture: A Reusable Past* (Washington, D.C.: Smithsonian Institution Press, 1995), 29–64.

regarded as sufficient or even appropriate as the basis of a book or an essay. Be aware of that.

Historians prize primary sources: They're the gold standard. Even an account by a proven liar is valued, because liars can be revealing in multiple ways – *what* they deny, *how* they deny, what they *don't* deny. Of course, it isn't always easy to know if someone is lying, or to know if the person recording an event really understands what was actually going on. But you've got to start somewhere, and primary sources are, by definition, there at the start.

And, again, this matters because of that problem of scarcity. Take the case of one of the most famous people in the history of the world, Genghis Khan. This Mongol tribal leader, whose life began sometime around 1162 and ended sometime around 1227, created the largest empire the world has ever seen, among other things laying the foundations of the Yuan Dynasty of China. Yet we know almost nothing first-hand about him. The closest thing we have to a primary source is the anonymously authored *Secret History of the Mongols,* an epic poem published decades after his death. (It was lost to the outside world for centuries, recovered by Soviet historians of China in the 1930s.) In the *Secret History,* Genghis Khan "speaks," in that we have direct quotes purportedly recording what he actually said. But since it was written so much later – and since much of the text is a celebratory, even fantastic, account of his exploits – it's not exactly an account we can call reliable in a modern sense. But it's the only thing we have, and using it, however carefully and inventively, is the work of anyone seeking to understand the man or his milieu.[2]

---

[2] *The Secret History of the Mongols: The Origins of Chingis Khan,* adapted by Paul Kahn and translated and edited by Francis Woodman Cleaves (Boston: Cheng and Tsui, 1998). Note that there are multiple translations of Genghis Khan's name; I'm using the one currently in most common circulation in American English. Also note, as I did when I looked at the copyright page for this book, that in this particular case we *are* dealing with a translation, which puts this primary source at one remove, and the edition that I – a non-Mongol historian – am using is itself an abridged version of Cleaves's more authoritative edition, published by Harvard University Press. If *you* were writing a big essay on Genghis Khan, this is the version you would ideally consult.

## Obscure References, Maine Events

Other times, primary sources are so cryptic that it's almost impossible to know what they're really saying. Almost impossible, that is, if you're not as gifted as Laurel Thatcher Ulrich. Take, for example, this September 4, 1788 passage from the diary of an eighteenth-century Maine midwife named Martha Ballard:

> Clear. Mr. Ballard [her husband] gone to Mr. James Pages on public business. Jonathan [her son] and Taylor went to see the Execution of Oneal. I have been at home. The Girls washt. Gilbreath sleeps here. The wife of Old Mr. Springer Departed this Life this morn.[3]

You undoubtedly regard this entry as terse to the point of impossible to understand. So did most historians who came across it before Ulrich began researching it in the 1980s (there are references to the diary by scholars as early as 1870). More obviously interesting was the diary of Martha Ballard's contemporary, Henry Sewell, a Revolutionary War veteran who lived in the same town. His diary records events like the visit of George Washington in 1789. Yet through painstaking detective work, Ulrich was able to take entries like these and open a startlingly clear window on early New England: its gender relations, its domestic economy, its legal practices, and much more. Ulrich built much of an entire chapter in her Pulitzer-prize winning book *A Midwife's Tale* on this slender thread.

It's important to note that secondary sources were essential to Ulrich bringing this primary source to life. It has become a truism, almost a cliché, in the acknowledgments of history books that authors stand on the shoulders of giants, and this is no less true of the very best ones as it is beginners like yourself. To take one small example: Ulrich situates the diary of Martha Ballard in an ongoing debate among women's historians about the nature and persistence of "separate sphere ideology," a kind of prevailing common sense among nineteenth-century men and women

---

[3] Laurel Thatcher Ulrich, *A Midwife's Tale: The Life of Martha Ballard, Based on Her Diary, 1785–1812* (1990; New York: Vintage Books, 1991), 72.

regarding the division of labor and gender roles.[4] Reading this scholarship allowed Ulrich to put Martha Ballard in a particular context – one that largely didn't exist before the 1970s. But it also allowed her to see that this scholarship didn't quite capture the nuances of her primary sources, which suggest *interlocking* spheres more than separate ones, and a rich blend of personal, familial, and economic ties. So, for example, "the girls" doing the laundry that Ballard refers to in the above diary entry include her own daughters as well as other young females in the town who learned skills, contributed labor, and stitched the fabric of the community together.

Sometimes a historian uses secondary sources to triangulate between himself, his sources, and other people who have looked at the same ones. Jack Weatherford, the distinguished author of *Genghis Khan and the Making of the Modern World,* began his research conscious of Genghis Khan's notorious reputation as a destroyer of societies – a reputation he suspected was not entirely correct. In examining accounts of the Mongol leader and *their* sources, he became aware that many of those who complained most bitterly about Genghis Khan were members of defeated elites who were often corrupt, inefficient, or lacking the kinds of skills he was in fact eager to promote and reward wherever he found them. This pattern allowed Weatherford to see *The Secret History of the Mongols* and related documents in a fresh, provocative light. Weatherford's work is also a reminder that good history is not only a matter of finding sources, but also judiciously sifting, choosing, and arranging them, a topic we'll look at in more detail in chapter 11.[5]

## Scarcity and Plenty

Sometimes, the truly imaginative dimensions of doing history are not about unearthing or reinterpreting obscure documents, but thinking about commonplace ones in new ways. In his

[4]  Ulrich, 76.
[5]  Jack Weatherford, *Genghis Khan and the Making of the Modern World* (2004; New York: Three Rivers Press, 2005).

prize-winning 2005 book *The Fall of Rome and the End of Civilization,* historian/archeologist Bryan Ward-Perkins challenges a view among recent historians of the late Roman Empire that the barbarian invasions of the third and fourth centuries were not catastrophic events in the history of West, but rather a more gradual, multicultural transition from ancient to modern societies. One of the ways Ward-Perkins makes his case is through pottery. Cleverly, he zeroes in not on the elite artifacts one can still find in great metropolises like Rome, but rather the ordinary cookware excavated from remote locations like Roman- and post-Roman Britain. Here, he notes, there was a drastic drop in quality by the seventh and eighth centuries, an unmistakable step backwards, a real decline in the quality of everyday life. Ordinary people simply lacked access to the durability and elegance of cookware of people in earlier times, when societies could sustain higher standards of specialization and distribute goods over a larger geographic area than was later the case. Of course, none of the creators or users of these pots and jars were likely to be thinking of posterity while making breakfast during or after the Roman Empire, any more than you're likely to think of a colander as a document of your life when you're boiling pasta. But an insightful historian can nevertheless use such material in revealing ways – and provoke us to see our own lives with a new sense of clarity (kind of amazing, when you think about it, that this colander came from China) and contingency (there may come a day when we'll consider ourselves lucky to get our hands on macaroni and cheese).[6]

I've been emphasizing the ways a scarcity of material is one of the major issues, if not problems, facing historians, but that's not the whole story. In fact it is sometimes, even often, the case that there is a lot to work with, and the challenge takes the form of conceptualizing a project in a way that it *can* be done using finite materials in a finite amount of time. (Amusingly, Laurel Thatcher Ulrich's grant application for the project that a decade later became *A Midwife's Tale* asserts that "a single source study

[6] Bryan Ward-Perkins, *The Fall of Rome and the End of Civilization* (2005; New York: Oxford University Press, 2006), 87–110; 184–7.

makes an attractive and easily definable summer project.")[7] Here, too, thinking through a problem imaginatively and conceptualizing in tight but resonant parameters is likely to count more than dogged research. A student of mine in a Civil War course was curious about how adolescents think about the Civil War – what aspects of it they tend to emphasize or overlook. Her primary source: YouTube videos. She identified dozens – a finite but sufficiently representative sample – in a paper that ultimately explored the way kids today focus more on the tragic dimension of lost friends than the glamour of war or issues like slavery. The key to that essay was her cleverness in the way she framed it.[8]

Still, no matter how clever you are, sooner or later – and it's much more likely to be sooner than later – you're going to test your vague notions by actually identifying and seeking out sources. How do you do that? I'm sure you already have some ideas, as you've been looking stuff up for much of your life. But it's worthwhile to now turn our attention to process and skills involved in successful research.

---

[7] Ulrich's 1981 National Endowment of the Humanities application can be found at http://dohistory.org/book/100_grantapp.html (accessed June 19, 2007).

[8] Lily Newman, "Learning about the Civil War from Sources of Questionable Credibility," an essay written for Jim Cullen's "The Civil War: A Study in Conflict" course, spring 2007. Cited with the permission of the author.

# Chapter 4

# Good Answers
# Begin with Good Questions

- Good students have answers; great ones have questions
  - A good question is answerable in more than one way
  - A good question to resonates beyond its immediate subject
  - A good question opens windows on past and present
  - A good question is answerable
- So what do I ask?

For a lot of people, getting an essay assignment from a teacher is one of the less pleasant moments in academic life. For one thing, it represents a looming burden on your time and energy: Even a fun essay (which some students regard as a contradiction in terms) is going to be a lot of work. But what may be worse is the sheer sense of anxiety: How are you going to do this? What does the teacher want? Will you have anything to say? And if so, can you really fill up X number of pages on the topic?

Perhaps inevitably, your initial – and, perhaps, unwavering – response to getting an assignment will be to focus on your *answer* to the essay question. This is as likely to be true of a specific query that your teacher gives you, as well as a more open-ended one where you choose your topic (a scenario you may regard as even more stressful). In fact, of course, your answer is going to matter a great deal, and it is entirely understandable, even legitimate, for you to focus on that. Besides, one of the best ways to discharge anxiety about a looming undertaking is to dive right into it. But in this chapter, I'm asking you to break that circuit and to pause for a moment, to step back. I want you to resist that impulse to begin researching and instead linger on a subject that may seem like a detour at best and a distraction at worst. That subject is questions: what they are, why they matter, and, in particular, what good history questions should do – which, by the way, is something for which you should hold your teacher accountable.

## Good Students Have Answers; Great Ones Have Questions

There are few things more central to the life of the mind than the ability to pose a good question. Good students have answers; great ones have questions. This is as true of mathematicians (what would it mean to have a numeric concept of nothing, of zero?) as it is painters (what should a picture be now that we have photography?). Good questions have the power to turn meaningless *information* into meaningful *answers*. And while answers have the power to change *what* you think, questions have the power to change *how* you think – or, even better, to *make* you think.

The power of questions takes on an even greater intensity in our lifetimes, sometimes dubbed the "Information Age." Though you may not often think about it this way, you now have more data at your fingertips than the wisest sages of earlier times ever dreamed possible. Actually, you have more data at your fingertips than many people born before 1960 ever dreamed possible. To be sure, much of that information is of poor quality, if not useless (see appendix C for more on assessing Internet sources). But it's been getting steadily better, and there's good reason to think that the contents of entire university libraries will someday be open to you via remote wireless access from a laptop computer, as will books as they roll off the presses (a phrase that may soon change from a factual description to a cozy metaphor). As many analysts of contemporary life have observed, the key to success in your life, academically and otherwise, is likely to be less about finding information than in knowing how to organize and use it. And the key to that will be asking yourself good questions, whether or not your teacher is doing so as well.

Nowhere is the role of a good question more decisive than in the field of history. If sources are the life blood, then questions are its heart, the engine that drives it. Sometimes those questions are broadly philosophic, like proverbial one of whether men make the times or times make the man. Others are perennials that are engaged over the course of generations, like the question of what caused the fall of the Roman Empire, or whether the British did more harm than good in their administration of India. And still others are highly specific, even idiosyncratic, like, "What do the inquisition records of an erratic sixteenth-century miller tell us about the inner life of ordinary people otherwise lost to history?" the topic of Carlo Ginzburg's path-breaking 1976 study *The Cheese and the Worms.*[1]

But what is it that makes a good question good? For starters, here are three criteria:

- **A good question is answerable in more than one legitimate way.** In the humanities, at least, good questions tend to be open-ended. There are cases where history resembles science, and a good question results in a single, unambiguous answer. "Did Julius Rosenberg, who was put to death in 1953 for treason, really cooperate with the Soviet Union, as alleged?" The answer, we now know (because after the Soviet Union collapsed its archives were opened) is "yes." For scholars of the Cold War, this was an important discovery. But there may be less to it than meets the eye – or perhaps it would be better to say that this answer only raises other, less straightforward, questions. Was Rosenberg's behavior with the Soviets truly treasonous? If it was, did it merit the death penalty? And what about his wife, Ethel, who was also executed? And their innocent sons, who grew up without them: Was their parents' death fair to them? (Is that a relevant question?) Scholars continue to engage these matters even after Rosenberg's role has been established. The mere fact that they *can* be engaged, that

[1] Carlo Ginzburg, *The Cheese and the Worms: The Cosmos of a Sixteenth Century Miller,* translated by John and Anne. C. Tedeschi (1976; Baltimore: The Johns Hopkins University Press, 1992).

reasonable people come to different conclusions, is a big part of the appeal of history, why people choose to do it. But not the only reason.

- **A good question resonates beyond its immediate subject and invites consideration of broader historical issues.** "Was Napoleon Bonaparte a tall man?" is not a particularly good historical question. For one thing, it's not open-ended: We know that compared with his contemporaries, at least, he was not. For another, no answer is likely to tell us much, with the possible exception of whether knowing would suggest anything about the role of height in the making of political stature (psychologists use the phrase "Napoleon complex" to refer to people who try to compensate for their lack of height with grand deeds). But a question about the nature and durability of Napoleon's political reforms in France is another matter. Your answer to *that* question – let's say it's something like "He illustrates the salutary effects of centralized power in bringing about decisive social change" – is likely to have implications that take us far beyond Napoleon, France, and the nineteenth century. The answer will be revealing because the underlying question is important and relevant. We might, for example, apply any answers we derive from a question about Napoleon to earlier French history or the history of another nation at the same time.

- **A good question opens windows not only on the past, but on the present as well.** This point follows logically from the previous one, but deserves separate consideration. Some historians caution against the danger of reading too much into history, and of drawing misplaced "lessons" from the past that get misapplied to the present (I mentioned this back in the introduction, in talking about the "Munich analogy," which led American policymakers to try and avoid the mistakes of the Second World War, only to plunge into the quagmire of the Vietnam War). To be sure, any sophisticated student of history is going to be aware that people of the past are both similar to and different than those of today. And when I say "different," I don't mean a simple inversion, like a suggestion that medieval Roman Catholics were serious about their religion while

Roman Catholics today are not. My guess is that medieval Catholics were serious, as we understand the term, in some ways and not others, just as some Catholics care a great deal about particular issues (like, say, abortion) that didn't really figure prominently in everyday medieval life. All this said, unless we see *some* connection between the past and the present, derive some notion of the way we might live in knowledge of the way others have lived, then history is simply not going to be particularly interesting. That's another reason why a question of Napoleon's height isn't especially compelling: even if it was a debatable question, it would be a moot one, because the answer wouldn't be relevant to our lives (except perhaps for small people with large, imperial ambitions).

There is a fourth criterion in what makes a good question, and for our purposes it is the most important, because it is the most directly relevant in the daunting process of writing a good essay: **A good question is answerable.** This is an assertion that is relative and needs to be put in context. In the broadest sense, the proverbial question of whether men make the times or times make the man is not a particularly good one, because there is really no way of really knowing with much confidence, though one might make a pretty good case study through a particularly vivid, illustrative example. Other questions may be less philosophical, but so complicated to answer that a historian will give the better part of his life trying to do so, as the legendary biographer Robert A. Caro is currently doing in his multivolume work trying to get to the bottom of the question as to who the thirty-sixth president of the United States, Lyndon Johnson, really was.[2]

You, by contrast, are probably thinking in terms of weeks or days (hopefully not hours). Still, the single most common mistake

---

[2]  Robert A. Caro's massive biography, *The Years of Lyndon Johnson*, is currently in three volumes, all first published by Random House: *The Path to Power* (1982); *Means of Ascent* (1991); *and Master of the Senate* (2002). As of this writing Caro is currently preparing a fourth volume on Johnson's presidency. They are magnificent books, the finest flower of historical biography – perhaps not coincidentally, written by a man who was trained as a journalist.

students make in beginning an essay assignment is in casting too wide a net in trying to answer a question. They'll want to tackle the legacy of racism in Africa generally rather than looking at a specific colonial experience in a specific place at a specific time. They'll want to answer the question of the legacy of the 1960s in American culture without specifying a particular subset of people in the sixties. This is often the result of misplaced anxiety about whether there will really be enough to say when trying to answer a tightly focused question. Yes, as I noted earlier, a scarcity of good sources can be a real problem in historical inquiry. But a good question will take that into account and frame the possibilities as well as the limits in a way that makes the whole process of producing an essay easier.

## So What Do I Ask?

Where do you get good questions? The answer is your sources (see chapter 3). Good questions do not materialize out of thin air. Sources, which we think of as material that provides information, are also crucial in providing questions. Only by delving into sources – into researching – can a question really come into focus. And as often as not, a good question is the result of a *process*. You examine a source and generate a question (What is this person really saying?); read some more and revise that question (maybe what I really should be asking is: What *isn't* this person saying?); read some more and discard that question (forget about the first person – what's this other guy saying?); read some more and perhaps resurrect the question in a new form (actually, I now see that the first one's silence speaks volumes); and so on.

So in an important sense you're right if you're impatient and want to jump as soon as you get an essay assignment. But the crucial point, one that's subtle but truly decisive, is the *way* you jump in. The trick at the outset is to not be on the lookout for answers, but rather for intriguing, answerable, resonant questions. This is true even when you're handed a question by a teacher: In an important sense you've got to make it your own by tweaking, revising, or challenging it in a satisfying way. (We'll talk more about this when we discuss defining terms in chapter 9.) Doing this will not only result in more creative and satisfying work. It will also make the whole process easier and more rewarding.

One last point: coming up with questions takes time. Again: it's a process more than a task. Trying to write an essay all at once is a mistake, because you short-circuit that process. Dipping into things, letting your brain digest them on a back channel while you put away your laundry, take a shower, or go out for Chinese food (where you may or may not discuss them with a friend) is really central to the experience. I'm not necessarily suggesting that you do *more* work, that you let an essay take over your life. I am saying that slow roasting is better than fried.

Now let's talk about how to begin researching questions *and* answers.

# Chapter 5
# Search Engines, Research Ingenuity

- Net gains – and losses
- Stacks of possibilities
- Going by the book
- Take note with notes

All right then: You accept that history is a worthwhile undertaking, understand the difference between a primary and secondary source, and are willing to think, at least initially, in terms of questions rather than answers. Now what? What's the right way to do research?

If only there was an easy way to reply. Certainly there are things you can do – I'm going to get to those almost immediately – but the first thing I want to make clear is that research is an art, not a science, and at its best is a habit you develop rather than a fixed set of tricks. Anybody can do research. And just about everybody does – looking up a number in a phone book or checking to see how a movie has been reviewed is nothing if not research. But there can be so much more to it than that. Researching skills are a form of power that can improve your work and the quality of your life.

## Net Gains – and Losses

Let's begin with a somewhat touchy subject: the Internet (for more on this, see appendix C). Most books of the kind you're reading, including this one at an earlier point in the discussion, will warn you away from basing your work on sources you find online. That's good advice, not only because the quality of what you'll find there will not always be good – a website like *Hakim and Angela's FABULOUS guide to the Prezidents* should not inspire confidence – but also because there's all kinds of material you'll never be able to read, much less know about, simply from a Google search. Using the Internet for academic work is a little like eating fast food: It's undeniably convenient and cheap, but it's not good for you (something you can sometimes tell pretty quickly). You've got to be willing to do a little exercise, mental and even physical.

That said, it's hopeless to expect you won't start with the materials closest at hand, and that almost inevitably will be the Internet connection on your computer. The first stop for many students is an encyclopedia, particularly Wikipedia, a multilingual, web-based, free content encyclopedia that its website claims is ranked among the ten most visited sites in the world.[1] Wikipedia is a collective enterprise, to which anyone can contribute. It has been the source of some controversy.[2] But as a tertiary source (which, as you may remember from chapter 3, is a general overview of a subject, usually compiled from secondary sources), it's often as good as anything you will find on the Internet. I myself

---

[1] http://en.wikipedia.org/wiki/Wikipedia. Accessed July 4, 2007.

[2] Controversies like vandalism of some entries and manufactured credentials by at least one writer led Middlebury College to ban students from citing Wikipedia in their essays, though many teachers there and elsewhere recognize both the implausibility of an outright ban and the utility of Wikipedia when used properly. See Noam Cohen, "A Contributor to Wikipedia Has His Fictional Side," *The New York Times,* March 5, 2007 and Noam Cohen, "A History Department Bans Citing Wikipedia as a Research Source," *The New York Times,* February 21, 2007. Both accessed at nytimes.com (July 4, 2007). I read both these stories in the newspaper when they were originally published. One of the wonderful things about the Internet is that I could recover them quickly when I realized they could help me with this chapter. I did not provide the entire URL, which would easily fill a line of text and be unwieldy even if you copied and pasted them in your browser, because I think you will be easily able to find them using the author and or title of the piece in an online *Times* index at home or through your school. (See appendix A for more on citation methodology.)

often use Wikipedia. But – and this is important – *I never rely on it as the final source of a fact or a quote for anything I plan to use in print.* For background information? Sure. As a source of ideas about how to organize material? Absolutely. (Wikipedia does a particularly nice job of providing outlines with major articles.) But for a fact or interpretation that will end up in something I write? Not unless I can confirm it with something more solid. The same is true of any other website that does not originate with a source I consider reliable, like a research university or a major national newspaper.

In the earliest stages of my research I'm also apt to use an online retailer like Amazon.com. That's not because I necessarily plan to buy lots of books. Nor is it because I expect to be able to read much of what I find, even though some titles have a "Search Inside" feature that will allow a user limited access to excerpts. And I by no means assume that a retailer will have many or even most of the sources on a topic in question. But that's precisely the point. A resource like Amazon will point out the most recent material I'm likely to be able to get my hands on. Much of what's been published in the last decade is likely to be in a library somewhere (more on that in a moment), and if it's brand new, I should be able to find reviews of it relatively easily – or, if it looks really good, to take the plunge and buy it.

There is one other form of shopping I can recommend doing from home, and that is a quick raid on the treasures of the United States government. The Library of Congress, founded in 1815 when Thomas Jefferson agreed to sell his collection to the United States after the government's library was destroyed in the War of 1812, is one of the great libraries of the world. While you can't check anything out of it unless you happen to be in Washington, DC, you can learn what's out there on just about any subject (though only someone really practiced in using the *Library of Congress Subject Headings,* available online and in bound form in most public libraries, will really be able to navigate the maze). Even better, the LOC (www.loc.gov) has particular collections, like its wonderful "American Memory" website, where you can find, and actually view, all kinds of primary source documents – letters, maps, photographs, sound recordings, and much more.³ Not all this material can be easily downloaded, but a lot of it can. And even more of it can be ordered as prints at relatively low cost. Since much of this material is in the public domain – it belongs to the people – you can pretty much do anything you want with it. I've gotten a lot of the illustrations for my books this way.

## Stacks of Possibilities

Preliminary moves with resources like Wikipedia and Amazon. com are particularly useful at that stage of your project when you don't even really know what you're looking for. They will almost inevitably present you with sources, ideas, or topics that simply had not occurred to you. And if you find yourself getting restless, even unhappy, that can actually be helpful. It should prompt you to ask: Why don't I like what I'm finding? What did I expect? If I'm not finding that thing, or that aspect of the thing, that I'm curious about, is it because there's a bona fide shortage of information? Or maybe I'm looking in the wrong place? Maybe I'm asking the wrong question?

This is one of those moments when it makes sense to finally venture outside for a trip to the library. There are all kinds of reasons to go there, some of which you can foresee, and some which you can't unless you actually go. Sometimes the mere fact of taking a break by walking over there will allow you to clear your head in a way that can break a mental logjam.

Another great reason to go the library: librarians. Librarians are one of the great, and underutilized, resources of academic life. They're professionally trained to look for sources, and they're

³ http://memory.loc.gov/ammem/index.html (accessed July 6, 2007). It's important to note that the LOC also affords access to resources that are not solely focused on the United States. See, for example, the "Global Gateway" on its home page or go directly to the site (http://international.loc.gov/intldl/intldlhome. html). You may also want to consult other national resources such as Britain's BUBL (http://bubl.ac.uk/).

usually eager, even happy to help. (Be nice to them! Not only is it good manners, but they're people you want to have on your side.) Librarians not only know their way around the place in a way you never will, but they're aware of the newest catalogs, databases, and sources. They may also be able to point you in the direction of material not immediately on hand, but which they can get for you, through interlibrary loan, for example. Though this may not afford you instant gratification – and you should be doing this work far enough in advance so you can afford a little time – interlibrary loans services are often admirably efficient. Don't be shy or skeptical about this. There's no guarantee of a quick payoff, but chances are good that you will learn something from a librarian that you'd know no other way.

One of the things a librarian is most likely to show you that you wouldn't otherwise know about are newly published reference books, which are usually shelved separately from other books in the library. Here you will find not only periodically updated general works like the *Encyclopedia Britannica* (which has a much better intellectual reputation than Wikipedia), but also specialized works such as *The Encyclopedia of American Cultural and Intellectual History*,[4] high-quality tertiary sources typically written by respected scholars that will provide you with an overview of a topic as well as bibliographies that can really get you started. The reference section will also house dictionaries, atlases, and collections of documents that can both help you focus a topic as well as identify important sources. Some of these materials might be available online; some not. Because they're in book form, they sometimes date more quickly than Internet sources (though Internet resources that are not updated can get pretty musty, too). Yet even a dated source can be useful, because older sources sometimes get lost in the publishing shuffle, and can be more useful than material that simply happens to be newer. Newer sources often refer to golden oldies, so having access to those oldies can be helpful.

---

[4] *The Encyclopedia of American Cultural and Intellectual History*, 3 vols. Edited by Mary Kupiec Cayton and Peter W. Williams (New York: Charles Scribner's Sons, 2001).

Here's another kind of source, typically secondary, that libraries are good for: periodical literature, i.e. magazines, journals, reports, and other materials that are issued at regular intervals. (Libraries can also be good, even uniquely so, in offering access to primary sources like newspapers, particularly old or discontinued ones, though as often as not you can access them from the websites of newspapers themselves.) For the purposes of academic work, there are two types of periodical literature. The first is the so-called popular press, which consists of magazines published for a general readership, such as *Time, Newsweek,* and *Rolling Stone,* though it also includes specialty magazines read by people to enjoy in their spare time, like *Popular Mechanics* or *Scientific American.* The second are scholarly journals, such as *The Journal of American History, Foreign Affairs,* or the *American Historical Review* (the major generalist resource of record for all kinds of academic history published in the United States). There's some overlap in these categories – *Scientific American* is not exactly light reading, and *Foreign Affairs* is a journal you sometimes find in an airport shop. In general, scholarly articles are more authoritative but also more technical than those in popular press, where articles are usually shorter and more vivid, a tradeoff for you to consider – one reason to look for both.

Before the diffusion of the Internet of the 1990s, all periodical literature was printed on paper, bound in large volumes every six months or so, and placed on shelves in row after row in the stacks, where much of it can still be found in any given library. To save space, some library systems transferred such material onto rolls of microfilm and sheets of microfiche, which can be read using specialized machines in libraries. A little later, some of it was transferred to newer technology like CD-ROM. Nowadays, a lot of it – *but not all of it* – can be accessed online. Some of it – *but not all of it* – can be accessed at home. But again, it's hard to get the lay of the land without actually visiting the library.

So how do you find these treasures? The answer is catalogs. For generations of readers of the popular press, the go-to source was – and, for material published before the 1983 remains – the *Reader's Guide to Periodical Literature* published by the H. W. Wilson Company (material published subsequently can be accessed online). These big green volumes, which hold a few months of listings for any given year, are organized alphabetically by subject. You sometimes need to think a little creatively about how to search for that subject – you may get better results researching an essay about the Great Depression by looking up terms like "Stock Market" and "Herbert Hoover" – but the *Reader's Guide* is a notably user-friendly index to what was published in the popular press for much of modern times. (What do I mean by "modern times"? I don't say. But the reference to the Great Depression, which began in 1929, gives you a clue.)

There are a number of print and electronic databases for scholarly periodical literature, some highly specialized. Some of these resources list articles. Some include abstracts, or summaries of articles, which can be helpful in telling you whether it's worthwhile to track down the entire piece. Sometimes, if you're lucky, you can get the entire text from an online database. The *Humanities Index* (called *Humanities Full Text* online) catalogs most major English-language historical journals, among others. I myself am partial to JSTOR (short for "Journal Storage") an online index begun in 1995 that offers access to full-text versions of articles from thousands of journals whose topics you can narrow or tailor as you see fit. The directions for using such catalogs are usually pretty obvious when it comes to simple searches. But they often have sophisticated tools that allow you to narrow your search, if you know what you're looking for – and you know what you're doing. Neither, of course, can be taken for granted, which is one more reason why making friends with a librarian can help. Once you've got a title, the name of the journal, and the date (maybe the page number, but you can probably do without it by checking the table of contents when you find it), you can wade into the stacks – very often, journals are arranged alphabetically by title – and retrieve the article.

## Going by the Book

Reference works, documents, and articles are all common and useful sources for academic essays. But the cornerstone of scholarship, for now, anyway, remains printed and bound books. Chances are that any good essay is going to rely on books, though those books may be of different kinds and found in different ways.

One of the most potent tools at your disposal is your school's Online Public Access Catalog, often called OPAC, which you can access from home or the library (though of course you can only get the books by heading to the stacks). In these and the above-mentioned databases, you can find sources using an author, title, subject, or keyword – this last option is particularly helpful when you lack complete information or are trying to cast a wider net. The great asset of a keyword search is that you're likely to get lots of returns, which is great if you're still thinking broadly. The great liability of a keyword search is, well, you're likely to get lots of returns, which isn't great if you're trying to narrow your focus. Sometimes a catalog's search engine will make a distinction between the exact title of a book or words in the title. The former will sharply narrow the search so that you only get what you're looking for. The latter will be helpful if you don't know or can't quite remember a title, or if there may be a handful of books with similar titles.

Spend even a few minutes in front of a library catalog, and you're likely to generate a number of books that might be useful for your purposes. Some will be primary sources. Some will be secondary. Some will be edited anthologies of either or both, consisting of chapters or excerpts from a series of writers on a particular topic. Navigate your way through the various screens to get the call number, either via the Dewey Decimal System or the more expansive Library of Congress method, and be sure to check for the availability (no sense in looking for a book that's been loaned out) and locations (check, for example, that the book isn't a reference title, or kept in a special collection, which means it won't be shelved in the main stacks). Then, armed with the call numbers, and a map or directions from that friendly librarian, venture forth into the stacks.

As you grope your way through the shelves toward the book or books you're looking for, you'll begin to practice the final, and one of the most important, of research techniques: shelf browsing. Very often it's books *near* the one you're looking for, which are classified by their topic, that are as likely to be helpful as what you think you want. Spend some time around such shelves. You'll learn a lot just by looking at spines. It's hard to say how long you'll need to spend in the stacks. Maybe a few minutes, maybe a few hours. You may well find yourself flipping through a few books to decide if you want them. At some point, you'll decide you have enough and will check out, photocopy, or take notes on what you need. *Be sure to generate a preliminary bibliography on anything you imagine yourself using, whether or not you're actually going to quote it.* (See appendix A, for information on vital data for bibliographies and footnotes.)

## Notable Discoveries

It's at this point that you may also begin to take notes. Note-taking is a highly personal, even idiosyncratic, activity, and one that you'll probably develop on your own if in fact you haven't already. Just keep in mind two things. The first is recording your sources in such away that you will be able to find them again if you need to, and putting them in an order – alphabetical, thematic, chronological, whatever – that makes sense to you. Some people make lists on their computers; others remain faithful to the old-fashioned technique of index cards, which are easy to carry and shuffle. Second, write down anything in a way that you might find useful, whether a summary of a document, copying down key passages, or even general impressions, including opinions. Don't worry about clarity or insight for anyone but yourself. Some experts on writing emphasize the importance of distilling material, of boiling it down to its essence, and if that makes sense to you, do so. But other people seem to relish, even need, to write down material as a way of absorbing it (this is why note-taking is often more useful than it seems to be compared with photocopied or downloaded material, which you simply don't engage with as deeply).

In any case, as I said, this is the point where you *begin* to take notes. The process will continue, and get refined, as you proceed and begin to get a better idea of what it is you really want to write about.

Indeed, at some point during or after the collecting stage, perhaps in between or after multiple trips to the library, you'll need to really settle down and not merely dip, but dive, into some of what you've collected. And along the way you'll need to step back and reflect on what you've read. But this is likely to be a different kind of reading than you customarily do, and it merits some attention. So we're going to give the matter its own chapter.

# Chapter 6

# How to Read a Book without Ever Getting to Chapter One

- Pressing matters
- Inside information
- Going back, going forward
- Topic-sentence hopping

"Don't judge a book by its cover," goes the old saying.

The old saying is wrong. You *can* judge a book by its cover, literally and figuratively. Not only can people do so; they're often right to do so. In a world of limited time and information – the world in which essays get assigned and written – you simply can't afford to give every book (or any other source) the same consideration. To be sure, there are *some* books that deserve careful study, and *any* book can surprise you with its depth or insight. The trick – and like most, it's one that requires attention to technique and disciplined practice – lies in knowing what to look for, along with the calibrated effort to take chances with investing time in some that may or not pay off. As with most things, it's a willingness to tolerate some waste of your resources, whatever they may be, that can both show you really care about something and explain your eventual success. If the matter in question is something you're doing more out of obligation than interest, it may be worth reminding yourself that cutting corners may prove to be short-sighted, and to remain open to the possibility of being pleasantly surprised. Open hearts make for open minds, in learning how to read books and much else.

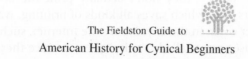

The Fieldston Guide to
American History for Cynical Beginners

Impractical Lessons
for Everyday Life

Jim Cullen

To illustrate my point about judging covers, let's take two I know a little about. The first is *The Fieldston Guide to American History for Cynical Beginners*.[1] This book's cover consists of the title and author on a plain white cover. On the bottom right-hand corner, there's a triangular illustration depicting a segment of the American flag. Though the art work is a bit rudimentary, I don't think of this as a particularly bad cover, really. But then, I wouldn't: I designed it myself.

Actually, I published the book myself. Not that you would necessarily know. The company on the spine of the book is iUniverse (www.iuniverse.com), out of Lincoln, Nebraska. iUniverse is an online outfit that, for a fee, will design and manufacture books for anyone with the money, and publish them on an

[1]  Jim Cullen, *The Fieldston Guide to American History for Cynical Beginners: Impractical Lessons for Everyday Life* (Lincoln, Nebraska: iUniverse, 2005).

"on-demand" basis – they don't actually print the book until anyone orders one, which saves all kinds of printing, warehousing, and other costs. In the days before the Internet, such author-financed houses were called "vanity" presses, since they did not publish books because they thought were important or profitable, but rather serviced those (aspiring writers, organizations seeking internal publications, rampant egotists) who wanted books they could literally call their own. Serious writers, editors, and readers look upon them with skepticism, and I will cheerfully tell you that they're usually right. Moreover, such people are usually skeptical about any book that emanates from Lincoln Nebraska, with the exception of one published by the University of Nebraska Press – a fine house, though not one, you could readily infer, with the same stature of, say, Harvard University Press. In my case, the book actually grew out of a website, *American History for Cynical Beginners*, which I developed for my students with the help of my school's technology specialist.[2] The book, financed by the school I work for, was meant to be an ancillary tool. So I don't mind telling you that I don't consider it my best work – though my real point is that you don't really need me to tell you in order to figure that out.

I did have an additional aspiration for *The Fieldston Guide to American History for Cynical Beginners,* however. I hoped that the idea behind the book – and at least some of its content – would attract a major publisher. I'm happy to say that proved to be the case. But now I need to tell you what that means.

## Pressing Matters

In the historical profession, there are two basic types of "major" publishing houses, with some overlap between them. The first are university presses. Generally speaking, the most prestigious scholarly work gets published by universities. Some of the big

[2] http://www.ecfs.org/projects/jcullen/. The site was designed with the help of Mary McFerran.

ones, like Oxford, publish in a great many intellectual fields. Others, like Duke University, specialize in particular areas, like literary theory. Generally speaking, anyone with hopes for a successful academic career needs to begin with publication by a scholarly press, ideally in a field in which a university press has a particular strength.

But that doesn't have to be the only place a scholar publishes. Regional journals, newspaper opinion pieces, and textbooks like this one are only some of the other venues in which a scholar's work might appear in the course of a career. But the other kind of "major" publisher for a historian – and *this* major is *more* major when it comes to money and possible fame – is "trade" publishing. In the United States, trade publishing is based almost exclusively in New York. Trade books are the ones that get advertised in newspapers and in store windows, and you can often find them in chain bookstores, where the hope is that they will bought by the general public. Sooner or later, most ambitious scholars try to publish with trade houses like Simon & Schuster, HarperCollins, Random House, or some of their subdivision imprints like Touchstone (S&S), HarperPerennial (Harper), or Vintage (Random House – Vintage is the gold standard in History). Such houses are not the only measure of quality, and they have disadvantages, among them that trade books go out of print quickly if they don't sell, while academic houses generally make a longer-term commitment to a book. But trade has the most prestige, and certainly trade books are very often attractively packaged.

Within trade history books, there's an official distinction between major scholarly books and "popular history." The former typically represents the top rung of a ladder a scholar climbs, beginning with specialized monographs (see chapter 2) and moving gradually toward expert status that culminates in the so-called "definitive" work on a topic. So, for example, a historian like James McPherson began his career focusing on the abolitionist movement in the Civil War era in the early 1960s, and wrote a steady stream of books culminating in his bestselling *Battle Cry of Freedom*, published by Oxford University Press (an academic publisher with trade muscle) which won him the Pulitzer Prize.[3] McPherson is regarded by historians as *the* authority on the subject. Popular history, by contrast, is often generated outside the academy altogether. It's written more for the edification and entertainment of armchair historians, who of course can be quite serious. So can popular historians, who often do distinguished work, even if they're sometimes regarded with disdain or even suspicion, in part because they rely more on secondary sources and are more attuned to present-day concerns. A good example is the late beloved historian Barbara Tuchman, who ranged widely across subjects that included the First World War, medieval Europe, and the American Revolution[4] – a mix that an academic scholar, who typically develops expertise in a single area, will rarely pursue. You'll probably find you like popular history more than academic history, but you'll also probably find that academic history will be met with more approval when you use it in an essay. The line between the two can sometimes blur, and you should develop independent judgment about which sources you think of as best. But that judgment should begin with a recognition of what might be termed the invisible class structure within the world of history books.

Which brings us to the cover of my previous book, *Imperfect Presidents,* a work of popular history.[5] Lots of people have had reservations about this book, myself included. But I got nothing but compliments for the cover, though of course it was done by a

[3] McPherson's first book was *The Struggle for Equality: Abolitionists and the Negro in the Civil War and Reconstruction* (Princeton: Princeton University Press, 1964). *Battle Cry of Freedom: The Civil War Era* (New York: Oxford University Press, 1988) followed *Ordeal by Fire: The Civil War and Reconstruction* (New York: McGraw-Hill 1982), a textbook that covers similar territory. Though McPherson followed up *Battle Cry of Freedom* with a string of successful books, it remains his signature work, and a generational landmark for Civil War scholars.

[4] Barbara Tuchman, *The Guns of August* (New York: Macmillan, 1962); *A Distant Mirror: The Calamitous 14th Century* (New York: Knopf, 1978); *The First Salute: A View of the American Revolution* (New York: Knopf, 1988). Tuchman's work has had little cachet in the academy, but she did win two Pulitzer Prizes and enthrall generations of readers.

[5] Jim Cullen, *Imperfect Presidents: Tales of Misadventure and Triumph* (New York: Palgrave, 2007).

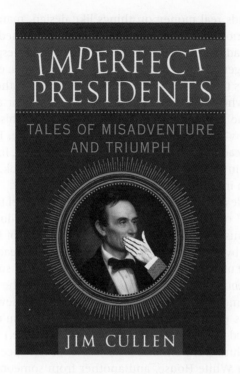

professional designer named David Baldeosingh Rotman. Rotman used a famous painting of Abraham Lincoln owned by the Corcoran Gallery in Washington, and covered Lincoln's mouth with an old-fashioned image of a hand to suggest that Lincoln had made a gaffe. It was a clever and playful encapsulation of the book, and one that beckoned the target audience – more curious generalists than serious scholars. Both images were acquired through Corbis, a well-known image archive, for which the publisher paid a fee.

*Imperfect Presidents* was published by Palgrave-Macmillan, an Anglo-American imprint that's part of Holzbrinck, a German conglomerate. Palgrave occupies a point on the spectrum between academic and trade, skewed a bit more to the former. I would not call it the most prestigious trade or academic house, though it is eminently respectable. It has a much higher profile than iUniverse, and it spends real money on things like design, manufacturing, and promotion. In order for this book to get published, a number of people had to believe in it – including editors, salespeople, and their managers, among others. At a university press, editors send manuscripts to one or more experts in the field on the subject in question, who judge, usually anonymously and for a small fee, whether the project deserves to get published. This process of "peer review" is central to the academic enterprise. But in both trade and academic publishing, a real, albeit limited, financial risk gets taken in deciding to commit to particular book, a decision undertaken in the hope of profit and/or prestige.

Both trade and academic publishers often put brief testimonials or "blurbs," on the back cover. In one sense, this doesn't mean much, because blurbs are almost always a matter of hype, often dashed off by friends who might not even have read the book. But they're often telling nonetheless, because they suggest what kind of friends the author has – how high up in the food chain she is. (Sometimes friends are also asked to review academic manuscripts at university presses – the process isn't always as high-minded there as it's sometimes made out to be.) In my case, I got one blurb from a friend who was a former speechwriter in the Clinton White House, and another from someone I used to work with who now runs a research center at Harvard. They were generous to lend me their good names.

Anyway, you see my point here: There's a lot going on with covers (front and back), and if you look carefully there are all kinds of things you can infer – or at the very least, ask. The same is true of the copyright page, which lists bibliographic information like who owns the right to the text (usually the author, though sometimes the publisher) and date of first publication. Who published this book? To which company does the imprint belong? How many editions has it been through? Again, such data can't tell you everything, and big numbers don't necessarily mean intellectual heft. Moreover, small or even vanity presses are sometimes the only source of information on a subject. And there's always the possibility that an obscure writer has more useful insight than a famous hack. So never let such tools of measurement substitute for active thinking.

## Inside Information

Most of the clues I've been talking about up to now are external indications of a book's potential value. They represent what publishing professionals think about a book more than what an author is actually saying. But once you flip your way into the interior, there are short-hand tools that can give you valuable cues about what a source might have to offer.

Take, for example, the table of contents for a book. A lot of the time, these are unremarkable. If you look, for example, at Adrian Goldsworthy's estimable 2006 biography of Julius Caesar, you'll see a division of the book into three parts corresponding to what he considers the most important phases of Caesar's career ("The Rise to the Consulship," "Proconsul," and "Civil War and Dictatorship"), each with about eight chapters covering segments of that phase. So in the case of the first section, we have "Caesar's World," "Caesar's Childhood," "The Young Caesar," and so on.[6] Nothing surprising about that – which tells us, for one thing, that this is not going to be some kind of revisionist approach to Caesar that looks at subjects like his attitude toward women or approach to barbarian peoples such as the Gauls (two subjects addressed by Goldsworthy, though certainly not his primary interest). That said, Goldsworthy doesn't exactly give us a generic division of Caesar's life either – "proconsul" is a term non-experts on Roman history are unlikely to readily recognize, and while someone with a general interest will learn soon enough what a proconsul does and why the job was important to Caesar, the expectation is that you're going to be willing to pay attention and pick such information up along the way – this isn't *Julius Caesar for Vaguely Interested Beginners*. A good table of contents will reveal such tendencies for those attuned to seeking them.

---

[6] Adrian Goldsworthy, *Caesar: Life of a Colossus* (New Haven: Yale University Press, 2006), v–vi. Goldsworthy, an Oxford-trained historian, had his book published simultaneously in the UK and the United States – an indication of its quality as well as the commercial appeal of its subject. (And the color photograph of the author on the back flap of the jacket also suggests a relatively high place in the publishing pecking order.)

Such clues can be especially valuable when a book is not organized in a straightforwardly narrative fashion but instead consists of a series of thematic chapters. A superb example is furnished by Gordon Wood's *The Radicalism of the American Revolution*, one of the most important books in the field in the last generation.[7] There are a number of things going on here (see right). As the title indicates, this is a book about the American Revolution, but it's pretty clear from this table of contents that you're not going to hear a lot here about Minutemen or Valley Forge. Nor are figures like Thomas Jefferson or John Adams fore-grounded – they're

part of the story, to be sure, but they're not primarily what Wood has in mind as an organizational strategy for the book. Instead, he's focused on ideas – the sequence of concepts that changed a set of British colonies into an independent nation.

The key word is *sequence*. If you look carefully, there's a real narrative embedded in this table of contents. Words in the first section like "Hierarchy" and "Authority," which imply order, give way to "truncated" and "loosening" and "revolution," suggesting transition and conflict. The final section foregrounds "Equality" and "Democratic." The last word – "order" – harkens back to the beginning, but the order now is a different kind of order, a middle-class, not aristocratic or hierarchical, order.

---

[7]  Gordon S. Wood, *The Radicalism of the American Revolution* (1991; New York: Vintage, 1993).

Which brings us back to that title. The word that really stands out is "radicalism" – the *radicalism* of the American Revolution. But what does Wood mean by the term? His radicalism is not that of Parisian mobs in the streets, a Latin American military junta, or a small cabal of Russian operatives engineering the overthrow of a tottering regime. It's "middle-class order," which conjures up images of shopkeepers, flower gardens, and lifestyles that your average Russian radical might regard as a bit bland. But getting *that*, Wood is clearly suggesting, is the truly revolutionary thing about the American Revolution. It's a rather conservative assertion to make – and Wood, many of his fellow historians (and non-fellows of the female persuasion) would say, is a fairly conservative scholar.[8] It's all there in the book, and if you went ahead and read it, I do believe you'd agree with me, even as we might debate some of the implications.

The point, though, is that you don't have to. The table of contents lays it all out in encapsulated form. Now, as I mentioned, this is a very important book, and anyone who considers themselves a serious student of the Revolution in this generation simply must read it, because there are details and nuances to Wood's discussion that are going to be part of the ongoing discussion of the period for the foreseeable future. But what if your essay is primarily on the colonial era? Then perhaps you'll zero in on the first section and skim the others.

But what if your essay is about Jefferson or Adams? Does the fact that they don't make it into the table of contents mean you're not going to find out anything useful about them? No, it does not. It's at this point you that should jump to the back

---

[8]  I myself was struck by an omnibus review (a review of more than one book) that Wood published at the time I was writing this book, in which he castigated contemporary historians for what he regarded as their excessive emphasis on slavery – an assertion I believe many of his peers would regard as misguided if not repellent, given what Wood himself acknowledges are centuries in which the topic was stinted if not ignored. See "Reading the Founders' Minds," *The New York Review of Books,* June 28, 2007, 63–7. Disagree or not, however, most professional scholars would acknowledge that *The Radicalism of the American Revolution* is a painstaking and elegant interpretation of the intellectual climate surrounding the event.

of the book and check the index. Adams is there all right – he pontificates on subjects that range from banking to Cicero, Julius Caesar's old friend and rival. So you can jump right in on page 318 or 204 and extract a nugget that might serve your purposes.

## Going Back, Going Forward

So far we've been dancing around the edges of books without ever really dipping our toes into the text itself. Taking the plunge is always an option – actually, at some point it's going to be a necessity if you're going plumb the depths that a good essay requires. But if you're still weighing whether or where to make your move on any particular source, there are two other places on the margins – one in the back and one in the front – where you can go for guidance about whether to make a commitment to a longer-term relationship.

Let's start in the back, with what is sometimes called the bibliographic apparatus – footnotes, biographies, abbreviations, and the like (sometimes it's also called the "back matter," which more broadly includes the index, sometimes the acknowledgments, and other documentation). In secondary sources, the sheer scale of such an apparatus is a sign of intellectual heft; it's not uncommon for major works of scholarship to have a hundred pages of footnotes or more. Bibliographies also often reveal important clues. How big are they? Are they subdivided between primary and secondary sources? Does the author use lots of archival records? Bigger isn't always better. Indeed, bigger can be overwhelming, which is why some histories, particular popular ones, use bibliographic essays, which are both readable and focused on the most important works. But even if you don't actually use the text of a book, the bibliography may clue you in to others that you will later find important.

The other place to look in any secondary source – probably the most important place to look, and the place that will be the locus of your own writing – is on the front end, specifically the introduction. The introduction is to history what the overture is to classical music: the place where themes get articulated and a (melodic, one hopes) interpretive line gets traced. Sometimes, a writer will open in an anecdotal way, with a little story that's meant to be illustrative. The extraordinary journalist/historian Adam Hochschild – who, perhaps not coincidentally, teaches writing at the graduate level – opens his vivid *Bury the Chains*, about the struggle to end the Afro-Caribbean slave trade, with twelve men in a printing shop. Hochschild is making the point that people can change the world; he invokes anthropologist Margaret Mead's famous quote that "a small group of thoughtful, committed citizens can change the world. Indeed it is the only thing that ever has."[9] In an important sense, the 300+ pages that follow amplify this message.

*Bury the Chains* is a trade book by an award-winning writer, and he means to entertain even as he instructs, the way the best popular histories do. This can make you a bit impatient when you're trying to skim a book, however, because what you really want are straightforward statements that explain what a book is about and how it's structured. That's why I began my book *The Art of Democracy* this way:

> *The Art of Democracy* was written as an introductory text of the U.S. experience with popular culture, an experience that shares important parallels with other societies, but one that has had a unique trajectory and influence. There has long been a need for this kind of book for the scholar, student, and general reader.[10]

There's some marketing and some historiography going on here. I wanted to make a case for what I regarded as the uniqueness of my book at the time I was writing it, and I wanted to justify its focus on U.S. popular culture both to keep the book of manageable size and to argue for a kind of American exceptionalism (an assertion which, by the way, I've retreated from in the

---

[9]   Adam Hochschild, *Bury the Chains: Prophets and Rebels in the Fight to Free and an Empire's Slaves* (2006; New York: Mariner Books, 2006), 1–8. Mead is quoted on p. 7.

[10]   Jim Cullen, *The Art of Democracy: A Concise History of Popular Culture in the United States* (1996; New York: Monthly Review Press, 2002), 2.

years since publishing the book). But the main thing I wanted to accomplish was to make as clear as possible as early as possible what it was a reader was looking at, and to assist that reader in getting where she wanted to go. The ensuing paragraphs of the introduction explained why the book was written, how it is structured and what the four main themes are. Sometimes an introduction will go even farther and devote a paragraph to each chapter of the book, identifying it in a topic sentence (more on these in chapter 10) and encapsulating it in a few subsequent sentences. Not exactly sexy, but undeniably practical – and when it comes to students in essay-writing mode, practicality matters most.

## Topic Sentence Hopping

One other thing you can do in an introduction – and, for that matter any other part of a great many books – is get a sense of what they're saying by skimming topic sentences. Topic sentences, which govern what a particular paragraph is about, are typically right at the beginning, with supporting material to follow. If you care more about what's being said than how, a good history book will allow you to glean a great deal from simply reading those sentences on any given page. Take, for example, this randomly chosen set of topic sentences from Charles Mann's *1491*, about the native peoples who lived in a North American region loosely designated "Cahokia" and built gigantic but mysterious mounds as a form of cultural expression:

> Nobody knows what these people called themselves or which language they spoke.
>
> Based around the Mississippi and its associated rivers, these societies scattered tens of thousands of mounds from Southern Canada and the Great Plains to the Atlantic Coast and the Gulf of Mexico.
>
> The earliest known examples appeared in [what is now] northeastern Louisiana about 5,400 years ago, long before the advent of agriculture.[11]

[11]   Charles C. Mann, *1491: New Revelations of the Americas Before Columbus* (2005; New York: Vintage, 2006), 286.

In between these topic sentences, we get lots of data, quotes, and other contextual information to support them. But we get the gist of what Mann is saying – who (to the extent we know), where, when – just by leapfrogging this way. If, in fact, we're really interested in Cahokia, we may want to pause here and look in detail at what he has to say. But if not, we may just want to move on. By the way, this approach to topic sentences can be useful in the writing process just as it is in the reading process, and it's a subject we'll return to in chapter 10.

There's more I could say here about how to skim, gut, limn (choose your verb) a source. And there's much here I don't discuss in depth, like how to case a primary source, which in general are much more resistant to such short-cuts, or how to detect flanking maneuvers in the acknowledgments of a book, which is often a site where egos get puffed, scores get settled, and the state of a field gets revealed. But I hope you get the main idea here, which is that sources are artifacts that can reveal a good deal more than what their authors explicitly say. Just having a consciousness of this fact is an important step in the making of a historian – or, for that matter, an educated person.

An important step, but only a first step. Let's take the next one.

# Chapter 7
# Analysis: The Intersection of Reading and Writing

- Making sense
- The choice factor
- Thinking with your heart

One night when I was in the early stages of drafting this book, I was channel-surfing on my recently acquired high-definition television, and came across *You've Got Mail*, the 1998 romantic comedy starring Tom Hanks and Meg Ryan, directed by Nora Ephron.[1] It was a happy moment. One reason is I could remember seeing the movie with my wife. Another is that the film, which I picked up midstream and ended up watching until it was over, has held up very well.

Another reason is that I found the movie to be a visually rich historical document. Set in what was then the present day of the mid-1990s, the movie offers a burnished picture of New York City (specifically the Upper West Side) during the prosperous years of the Clinton era. At one point Ryan's character, the owner of an independent bookstore threatened by the chain owned by Hanks, observes that she didn't vote in the mayoral election of 1997, in which Rudolph Giuliani was running for a second term, which had ironic relevance for me, since Giuliani was running for president as I watched the movie nine years later.

[1]  *You've Got Mail*, written, produced and directed by Nora Ephron, Warner Bros., 1998.

*You've Got Mail* is actually a digital-age remake of the 1940 film *The Shop Around the Corner,* which also has a bookstore backdrop (albeit in what appears to be Budapest) in which two characters conduct a passionate romance by mail, never realizing that they're working in the same store. Besides updating this scenario with New York style capitalism, writer/director Ephron put a modern-day spin by having the two characters be commercial rivals who don't recognize each other's e-mail addresses. The title of the movie refers to the slogan subscribers to AOL hear when they log on and have messages in their in-boxes. That very phrase is now a historical artifact of the 1990s. So are the jacks these sleek young people have coming out of their laptops – these days we go wireless through wi-fi connections.

I do have a point in all of this beyond illustrating the way history threads through ordinary everyday experiences like seeing an old movie on TV. ("What's a high-definition television?" your children may ask you someday.) And that involves the decisions that get made. One of the most enchanting things about *You've Got Mail* is the way the two skilled lead actors – who teamed up previously in 1990 for *Joe Versus the Volcano* and again in 1993 for *Sleepless in Seattle* – dramatize the solitary act of reading their e-mail. They smile; they frown; they gesticulate silently while they read and imagine the person who sent them a message. When they respond, they make false starts, they pause, and they chuckle as they "listen" to themselves or figure something out in the process of writing. The seemingly "simple" acts of reading and writing – which here are so tightly intertwined as to be inseparable, like conversation – are an intense experience that's emotional, intellectual, and even physical all at once. It's all action, process, something that they *do*.

## Making Sense

In a way, writing an essay is like that. What you write is deeply bound up in what you read, and when you really hit your stride, it too can even be an emotional and physical experience. (I myself am a pacer when I'm deep into a writing session – I get up and walk in circles while I think about what comes next.) Above all, this kind of work is about *doing*: It is not a passive experience. It's a different thing than simply sitting back and reading a book on the beach or watching a movie on the couch – as different as watching a game and playing in one.

*The process of making sense – of sense as something that you* **make**, *by reading and writing and thinking – has a name in the academic world. It's called* **analysis**. *Analysis is the value-added that you as a reader/ writer bring to the table, what* **you** *contribute.*

At this point it may be helpful to say more about what analysis isn't as well as what it is. Repeating a set of facts – like, say, stating that Sydney has the largest population of any city in Australia, followed by Melbourne and then Brisbane – does not constitute analysis.[2] Nor, strictly speaking, does mere description add up to analysis. If I tell you that Melbourne was founded in 1803 by British settlers, that it historically has attracted Greek, Italian, and Jewish immigration, and that it is the home of a relatively prestigious national university, I'm not making an analytic statement, either. Actually, given that these are fairly well-known facts to many Australians, I'm not even saying something that requires a footnote, any more than saying Tom Hanks is a famous American actor does. And mere opinion – "I think Melbourne is the nicest city in Australia" – doesn't count, either, because it's a bland and even meaningless statement without any sense of what I mean by "nicest."

All that said, there's raw material for analysis here. If I tell you that "Melbourne is the nicest city in Australia because it has a rich heritage rooted in its demographic diversity, and though it is smaller than Sydney it nevertheless deserves more consideration than it gets as a cultural capital," we're beginning to get somewhere analytically. Facts are being *used*; description is being *filtered*; opinions are being *defined* and *justified*. You can see a (perhaps fallible) mind at work. There's no litmus test for analysis, though with experience you'll recognize it when you see it.

---

[2]  I base this statement on data I found at http://www.citypopulation.de/Australia-UC.html#stadt_gross (accessed August 2, 2008).

Of course, it's one thing to recognize analysis. It's another to produce it. Analysis is one of the more neurologically complex feats you can perform in your life. The ability to do it is what people typically mean when they call somebody "smart." So where, as a writer poised to make the transition from research to writing, ready to take any notes you may have collected and turn them into something resembling an essay, do you begin?

## The Choice Factor

Here's where: by focusing on choices. The essence of history, both as a written experience and lived experience, is choices. Pay attention to the choices, and analysis will follow.

Choices are central to any number of human experiences, of course, particularly the arts. Let's go back to *You've Got Mail* for a moment. When Tom Hanks and Meg Ryan were pretending to respond to those e-mails, they were acting in one of any number of ways they might have done. They might have remained perfectly still while they were reading, for example. Or they might have burst into song and dance (which is what they would have done if writer/director Nora Ephron was making a musical). But Hanks and Ryan didn't act in these ways. Or, at any rate, we didn't *see* them act these ways – I assume they rehearsed their scenes and shot them multiple times, just as their characters erased and rewrote their emails (and just as I erased and rewrote sentences from the very book you're now reading). In the end, though, there was a final cut, a *version* of the story – in this case a story that had been told back in 1940 with a different cast and a different setting – and that's the version I saw in a multiplex theater in 1998 and again on my television in 2007. When I tell you that I really liked Tom Hanks and Meg Ryan in that movie, when I say that I thought they did some really good acting, what I'm really saying is that I liked the choices they made at a series of moments, and the choices Ephron and other filmmakers made in producing the document we know as *You've Got Mail* (which, by the way, was a clever choice for the title of the movie). In all kinds of ways that include the roles he accepts, the way he portrays them, and the way he talks about them when I see him promoting his latest movie, Tom Hanks is a really good chooser.

But he's an actor, not a historian.[3] Actors characterize people in real time; historians characterize times (and people) from the past, manipulating that characterization through compression or segmentation. An acute reader of history is no less attentive to the choices of a historian than an acute moviegoer is to the choices of an actor.

Noticing those choices, imagining alternatives to those choices, and assessing the utility, grace, and validity of those choices are important steps on the road to incisive analysis. Consider this passage on the coming of the Civil War from a highly regarded biography of Abraham Lincoln published in 1945:

> In the year of our Lord 1860, the United States was at peace. In all that was sound and fundamental, in every instinct that was normal and sane, the people of America, and their genuine friends abroad, wanted that peace to endure.[4]

Well, maybe. But one could also describe the same moment this way:

> In the year of our Lord 1860, the United States was on the brink of disaster. False voices of moderation, conflating the status quo with sanity, and overlooking crimes against humanity, counseled business as usual at home and abroad, wanting an illusion of tranquility more than a just peace.

I hope that James G. Randall's choices in the first passage come into sharper focus when juxtaposed with my alternative. I'm not particularly interested here in criticizing Randall, who

---

[3]  Not that these categories are mutually exclusive. See, for example, "National Character," my piece on Irish actor Daniel Day-Lewis as U.S. historian in the July 2007 issue of Common-Place (http://common-place.org/vol-07/no-04/school/).

[4]  James G. Randall, *Lincoln the President: Springfield to Gettysburg* Vol. I (New York: Dodd, Mead, 1945), 1.

was the pre-eminent academic Lincoln biographer of his day, though I will say that I do believe he had blind spots, and that other historians of his time, in the academy and outside it, would agree.[5] What I really want to call attention to, though, are two different sets of priorities. Randall, who lived through the Great Depression and the Second World War, and who viewed ideological conflict as divisive and destructive, subscribed to what has come to be known as "the blundering generation" school of Civil War historiography that blamed inept politicians for triggering the war. He regarded activists who sought to end slavery, however well-intentioned, as misguided extremists who could be as dangerous as Nazis or Communists. But an abolitionist like Frederick Douglass, in 1865 describing the coming of the Civil War, or a Civil Rights-era historian describing the coming of the Civil War in 1965 (like James McPherson, discussed in chapter 6) would render an account closer to the alternative I've fashioned here.

Inexperienced students of history sometimes make the mistake of thinking that history is primarily about telling stories factually. Facts are certainly important; you can't write history without them. But the issue is always: *which* facts? Arthur M. Schlesinger, Jr.'s Pulitzer Prize-winning *The Age of Jackson*, also published in 1945, is a masterpiece of style and diligent research. But the word "Indian" can't even be found in the index, and he gives a single paragraph to the removal of Cherokees from Georgia (other tribes and other states go unmentioned).[6] Historians today consider what we call "the Trail of Tears" to be one of the most important and shameful episodes in Jackson's presidency, and no account of the period would be regarded as complete without it.

Of course, in the context of twentieth-century historiography, Schlesinger was hardly unusual in stinting the role of Native Americans – an important indication that choices themselves

---

[5]   For more on Randall's biography and its place in Lincoln historiography see Jim Cullen, *The Civil War in Popular Culture: A Reusable Past* (Washington D.C.: Smithsonian Institution Press, 1995), 50–64.

[6]   Arthur Schlesinger, Jr., *The Age of Jackson* (Boston: Little, Brown, 1945). Schlesinger discusses the Cherokees on page 350.

are historical artifacts of a sort. Indeed, you can't really call something a choice if a person has no consciousness of it, which is why historians remind us to respect the "pastness of the past," and not to impose our standards now on people then. I'm an admirer of Arthur Schlesinger Jr., an erudite man who lived a long and productive life that including serving as an advisor to President John F. Kennedy as well as writing a thoughtful critique of multiculturalism.[7] It's in that context that I'm making the judgment – the choice – to criticize him (mildly) for his lack of attention to Native Americans in *The Age of Jackson*, rather than simply say he didn't know any better.

Again: We're talking about choices here, and a choice is an active decision. Merely noting that different people have different opinions about different things, and that what you believe really depends on your perspective – this is exactly how too many students I encounter seem to think – is not analysis. It's not really even thinking. Analysis requires engagement. And engagement requires something that's often missing in discussions of history: emotion.

## Thinking with Your Heart

This may strike you as counter-intuitive advice. Actually, it may strike you as wrong-headed advice: Historians typically see themselves as rational, cool-headed people, and the word "emotional" in this context is not only negative, but the very opposite of analytical. But as any psychologist will tell you, emotions lie at the heart of any rational response to the world – you would have to be insane not to feel fear as a bear charges toward you in the woods – and most historians acknowledge that feelings powerfully shape the spirit (though not typically the content) of their research. No one grapples with a subject like the Holocaust feeling indifferently about it, and anybody who did would produce work that was boring – or offensive.

---

[7]   Arthur Schlesinger, Jr. *The Disuniting of America: Reflections on a Multicultural Society* (New York: W.W. Norton, 1992).

This is not to say that emotions should *rule* your work. Nor am I saying that an opinion is valid simply because it is strongly held (*why* it's strongly held, what the strength of the opinion *reveals* about you, may well be more important). You don't choose how you feel. You *do* choose what you do with how you feel, and that does not always mean simply accepting or reporting that feeling. Intense emotion can certainly focus your thinking, but that's also a problem, because it narrows your perspective. And your credibility, something we're going to be talking about a lot in coming chapters, depends on some degree on detachment, on your ability to separate yourself from your feelings and view matters from more than one point of view. Yet even here, it's often impossible, and undesirable, to seal off emotion entirely. Reading and writing history are very often imaginative acts. Grappling with the Holocaust involves trying to understand why anyone would want to kill Jews, which in turn might well mean sympathizing with a Nazi, as more than one Jewish historian has done. Perhaps you find such a notion scary. But powerful feelings, pleasant or not, are likely to drive your essay forward.

How? Through questions. If feelings are the fuel, then questions are the match, the spark that ignites the essay. As you assess your most important sources, ask yourself two in particular: "What am I feeling?" and "Why am I feeling this way?" The answers are, of course, likely to be subjective. That's a good thing. Subjective feelings, by definition, are not universal; they require some explanation to be comprehended by those who do not share them. And explanation is the essence of analysis. Telling why – why something works or doesn't, emotionally or otherwise – involves making observations, arranging information, and offering interpretations. You're creating a product, and that product is analysis. And that analysis, in turn, is something you and others can do something with, like accept, reject, debate, or otherwise evaluate it.

We've reached a crucial turning point. Good reading involves paying attention to a source on that source's terms – *what* it says, *how* it says, *why* it says what it does. But good writing involves talking about a source on *your* terms, making sense of sources in ways that respect them even as you assert your own identity.

67

In so doing, you create something – a new source – that another reader can use for her own purposes. This is why writing is both a deeply personal, and a deeply communitarian, act. Like getting and sending really good e-mail.

Different communities have different neighborhoods, and different rules, formal and informal. Right now, we're in academic essay territory. So now let's turn our attention to a little code – or, more accurately, a formula – that will both allow you to express yourself and fit in at the same time.

# Part II
# Writing to Get Read

# Chapter 8
# Making a Case:
# An Argument in Three Parts

- Reading your reader
- Writing the equation
  - The question
  - The thesis
  - The motive
- Arguing about time

Historians argue. A lot. Some would say that's all they do.

Of course, the word "argument" doesn't quite have the same meaning in history, or the academy generally, that it does in some sectors in everyday life. At home, the word has negative connotations; an argument is something your parents have that you wish you didn't have to hear. There are people, like sports fans, who relish arguments: Can you be a truly great quarterback if you never win the Super Bowl? Is LeBron James as good as Michael Jordan was? Sports arguments can sometimes get nasty. But they're not quite the same kind of argument that historians make (even if sometimes they too can get nasty). They're the kind you should be learning to make at this point in your academic career.

Every so often in reading a student essay, I encounter a sentence in the introduction that says something like, "In this paper I will prove that …". But in history, as in most disciplines, one rarely proves anything. That's not even typically the goal. The real goal is *persuasion*. It's to make a statement about that past that isn't, or even can't, be proven, a proposition that you know at the outset not everyone would agree upon – one that's argu*able* – and to convince your reader to say, in effect, "Yeah, that's right." Your reader's assent may be a matter of thinking, "I didn't think the way you do before reading your essay, but now that I have, you've really changed my mind." Or it might be, "I always suspected as much, but you've given me reasons to think so that I never quite articulated for myself." Or it might be, "Wow: I never thought about this at all before. But now I see that it matters, even if I'm not sure I agree with your take on it." Any form of these counts as success. Depending on the circumstances, you might be happy with less: "Well, no, I still don't agree with you, but I can see you have a point." Or even: "I'll give you points for cleverness, anyway." What you really don't want to do is offend or confuse your reader: "Wow – that's really self-indulgent." Or simply: "What's your point?"

## Reading Your Reader

Which brings us to the very first question you should consider when you begin to write: "Who's my audience?" You know perfectly well that you don't talk to your grandmother the same way you talk to your best friend, a college admissions officer, or your six-year-old cousin. You calibrate your speech instinctively. But in writing, where you're not typically in the presence of the person you're addressing, you have to *imagine* your reader. The better you are at that, the better your essay will be.

Of course, being good at that means paying attention – and not just when you get the essay assignment. Real students are always reading, even when the texts happen to be people. I sometimes hear students complain that different teachers all seem to want different kinds of things from their students. To which I say: Hello! That's the point. There is no one way to write. Good writing is inherently flexible. I'm not writing for you right now the way I would for a scholarly paper to be delivered at an American Historical Association conference. If I did, you'd ignore me.

Professional writers have the tricky task of trying to identify approaches to writing that will attract relatively large numbers of readers. Your task, by contrast, is simpler. You typically have a primary audience of one: your teacher, along with maybe a parent and a peer or two. A good teacher will give you *some* (not complete) idea of what she thinks makes a good essay, an idea that's rooted in a pedagogical context, whether that context is a subject you're studying, a question you're being asked, a skill you're practicing, or all three. But whether or not you actually get such guidance, you should be asking yourself: Who is this teacher, really? What does she value most? Does she care about whether I use the first person, or what form of citation to use, or how long the essay is? You could of course ask. But there are other things you may just have to infer, like how casual a tone you should use, or how boldly you should state your opinion.

You of course have your own ideas, your own values, and maybe by this point even your own style, and you shouldn't disguise your feelings or mislead your teacher. But the fact is that you *are* a student, and at this point of your development the goal should be less a matter of principled stands about style (content is a different matter) than gaining experience in writing different ways for different people in the process of developing a voice that's authentically your own – a voice that's yours whether you whisper, shout, or otherwise modulate it.

Considering your audience is a very important question, and a good way to begin. But after making a preliminary assessment of who's going to read your work – a sense of scope, pitch, and size for the argument you're going to make – it's one best put aside until the revision process. You've spent some time thinking about what your sources are saying, and you've considered, in general terms, what you think your reader wants to hear. Now it's time to focus on what you want to say – your argument.

## Writing the Equation

And this brings us to what I regard as one of the core concepts of this book – more specifically, the formula that I believe best allows students to articulate, and then execute, arguments. Here it is:

**Question + Thesis + Motive = Argument**

People write in different ways, and no advice anyone gives you should be viewed as absolute. But *my* argument is that conceptualizing an essay at the beginning of the writing phase in this way – deciding what each of the three elements on the left-hand side of the equation will be and distilling them each into a single sentence – will make the right-hand side of the equation both easier to produce and better than it otherwise would be. Now let's take each of these elements in turn.

**The Question.** If you've read other parts of this book already (particularly chapter 4), you know that asking questions is an important part of the process right from the very moment you get an assignment. But while it's one thing to ask questions in the course of researching an essay, it's another to decide what *the* question will be. Not that this has to be final until the very end. But in order to get writing in earnest, you're going to need to have some sense of what we might call the core question (subject to revision) that you're going to be addressing. The clearer you are in your own mind about this the more likely you are to be successful.

In the early stages of an assignment, your question is more likely to be in the realm of a topic than a specific query. You may be thinking something like "I'm interested in what happened when the Japanese occupied China in the 1930s" or "I'm curious about how Europeans justified their racism toward Africans in the late nineteenth century." As you delve into your sources, these general interests should gradually get more specific. You'll begin to realize that the quest for raw materials powerfully shaped Japanese foreign policy at least since the time of the Russo-Japanese War of 1904, or you'll encounter an amazing book like Adam Hochschild's *King Leopold's Ghost*, and be stunned by the sheer scope of the lies in the Belgian administration of the Congo.[1] You'll poke around some more, shift your focus, and eventually feel like you have enough information to both ask, and begin to answer, a question like "What role did petroleum play in the defeat of the Japanese empire?" or "How did modern techniques

---

[1] Adam Hochschild, *King Leopold's Ghost: A Tale of Greed, Terror, and Heroism in Colonial Africa* (1998; New York: Mariner Books, 1999).

of public relations affect the campaign to reveal King Leopold's atrocities?" The goal is to find that sweet spot between asking a question that's specific enough for you to answer well, without being so specific that there's only one real answer that isn't particularly interesting (which is to say that it isn't particularly arguable). "Did the King's representatives say factually inaccurate things in the effort to deflect attention from what he was doing in his personal fiefdom?" isn't a great question, because we already know they did. Asking if the Belgians were evil people isn't a good question either, because it's really broad (in terms of who you mean, and what you mean by a theologically fraught term like "evil") and because it's not particularly relevant (we're both talking about a subset of Belgians – and, at the same time, anyone who has ever lived in a society with imperialistic tendencies). But a question doesn't have to be perfectly formulated to make progress on your essay; indeed you may not be able to improve your question until you start actually writing a draft.

   **The Thesis.** Simply put, the thesis – a word you've probably heard a lot already over the course of your schooling – is your answer to your question. But I'll give you a more pointed definition: *A thesis is a not-obvious, but true, assertion.*[2] When I say "true," I don't mean it in a factual sense, or as a hypothesis that can be tested in a laboratory. I mean it as something I and others believe to be the case, something we should accept, and act upon, as a valid description of the way the world really works. A statement that Avril Lavigne is a successful Canadian pop star is not an especially arresting thesis. Saying that Lavigne became a pop star thanks to the influence of her history teacher is a very interesting thesis (to me, anyway), but unfortunately is not one where you're going to be able to find much evidence (and evidence, alas, is one of those things every good argument is going to have to have in

---

[2] I learned this definition from Gordon Harvey, associate director of the Expository Writing Program at Harvard University, as part of my training when I began teaching the there in 1994. Much of the conceptual framework of this chapter rests on his insights, which I am filtering through the disciplinary lens of history. For more on his conceptual framework, see his pamphlet *Writing with Sources: A Guide for Students* (Indianapolis: Hackett Publishing Company, 1998).

abundance, as we will discuss in chapter 11). Saying that Lavigne is not your typical pop star, in that she captures the joy and anguish of adolescence with an uncommon degree of authenticity and insight – now that's a thesis. And if you make that case successfully, by defining what you mean by words like "authenticity" and "insight," and in giving real evidence to support your point, you might even get your reader not only to think, "Yeah, that's true," but go out and download some Avril Lavigne music. And this brings us to the final component.

**Motive.** This is a complicated concept, and it's often one that really only fully comes into focus at the end of the writing process (see chapter 13). But it's worth thinking about now. Simply put, a motive is a reason why the thesis matters. (Some people call it the "So-what question.") All right, then: You're telling me that Avril Lavigne is really an intriguing and revealing artist. And you've given me evidence that "So Complicated" vividly captures adolescent angst. But why does this matter? Why should I care? As I've already indicated, one answer is that a persuaded reader would acquire some Lavigne for a music collection. But just as there are any number of possible theses for an argument, so too are the multiple possible motives. Maybe your larger point isn't so much about Lavigne herself, but the role of females in popular music generally. Or maybe you're advocating for the use of pop music as a kind of diagnostic tool for recognizing personal distress. Or maybe you've realized that all the truly emotionally daring rock stars of the last few decades – Joni Mitchell, Alanis Morrisette, and Lavigne – have been Canadians, who we chauvinistic Americans too often consider bland people.

The difficulty with motives is that much of the time they're either buried in your consciousness or a visceral emotion you haven't quite explained to your own satisfaction. A motive often drives your work, but you yourself may not really understand how or why until you've actually worked through your material and written a rough draft. Very often motives don't really snap into place until the end.

There are people and situations where the motive seems to come first, a powerful feeling or attitude toward a subject that you feel you know from the start ("I want people to understand what just how overrated Avril Lavigne really is.") Such a feeling, though, suggests something may not be quite right with your process. On the one hand, a strong feeling can easily turn into a bias, which can blind you to relevant evidence and/or cause you to lose credibility with your reader. On the other hand, if a motive is really that sharply etched in your mind, maybe it should really be a thesis rather than a motive. You can make "Avril Lavigne is an overrated artist" your thesis, and then come up with a motive for it – like, say, an assertion that rhapsodic reviews of her music (which you've gleaned through research) show a marked tendency to celebrate the mere expression of an emotion as art, when it's really little more than juvenile venting. Don't be afraid to take your most focused, ambitious proposition and make it your thesis for fear that you won't have a motive. A useful implication can always be drawn from a strong idea.

## Arguing About Time

As my example with Avril Lavigne indicates, the construction of arguments is not specific to history. It isn't even specific to academic life – if you look hard at a movie, a novel, or a television show, you can often detect an underlying argument consisting of a question, thesis, and motive as defined here, even if it gets expressed in a different way. (Actually, works of art often have multiple arguments, which is why they're so interesting and worth writing about.) But again: We're in history land. That means that arguments are about time in some fashion, and in the case of a motive, you're drawing a conclusion from your thesis that pertains to the past, the present or both. You're saying, "If you agree with me, then you're going to see the past differently than you did." You may even be going a step further: "And if you see the past differently, that means you're going to understand the present differently too – and make different choices than you currently do."

Now that you have at least a vague idea of what a question, thesis, and motive are as they relate to an argument, my advice to you is that you take some time really tinkering with each element – moving them around, distilling them, rearranging them, etc. – until each one is a concise string of words no longer than an average sentence. Your goal is to get to a point that looks something like this:

**The argument for my essay on Japanese imperialism**

**Question**: What role did petroleum play in the defeat of the Japanese empire?

**Thesis**: The unsuccessful bid to control access to raw materials, petroleum in particular, proved far more decisive in the failure of the Japanese empire than the military prowess of Japan's opponents or the political decisions of the government between 1931 and 1945.

**Motive**: Voters, politicians, and historians too often overlook the way the politics of oil has affected – and does affect – the fate of nations.

If you get to a point where you have something like this – maybe even making it a document that you print on a sheet of paper – it can be your lodestar, your point of reference, as you move from the forest of argument into the trees of evidence, topic sentences, definitions, and some of the nuts and bolts discussed in ensuing chapters of this book. You may find yourself pulling back and looking at the argument, and, feeling dissatisfaction, tweak it a bit before moving forward again. You will in any event have a frame of reference, a base, from which to work and which will keep you on the straight and narrow.

You'll have something else that you need, too: the raw material for the most important piece of any essay – its introduction.

# Chapter 9
# Defining Introductions

- Introducing the question
- Introducing the thesis (and motive)
- Introducing the key term
- Introducing the premise
- Watch your language: diction

I feel pretty confident when I tell you that no element of any essay you write is going to give you more trouble than the introduction. Introductions are where your reader begins an encounter with your work. But they're almost always – no matter in what the sequence you actually draft an essay – among the very last things you're fussing with at the end. Still, as I indicated in the last chapter, it's a good idea to have the general pieces of your intro in place early on in the writing process, and so I think this is a good point in the conversation to take them up as a topic.

A good introduction, whether in an essay, book, or other expository medium, should do two things. First, it should convey in a fairly concise form – which in the case of an essay is typically less than a page – just what the author's argument is. (This is certainly true of the question and thesis; motive, as we will discuss, is sometimes more hinted at than stated, and it often only emerges fully in the conclusion.) The second is that the argument should be conveyed in a manner that will attract a reader, whether in the arresting formulation of the thesis, the notable clarity of the language, or some other quality. This is often more a goal than a reality, and it's not one, in any case, that you can worry much about in the early going. But it's nevertheless worth keeping in mind, as long as you don't let it paralyze you. At this point, getting something down is more important than getting something right.

In the last chapter, I counseled you to develop your question, thesis, and motive into three discrete statements. This is because they not only constitute your argument in the form of a road map; they also form the core of your introduction. But that core needs now needs to be refined. The discrete pieces need to be connected to each other, and placed into a context that your reader can readily apprehend.

## Introducing the Question

Take, for example, your question. It is theoretically possible to simply begin an essay with a query: What role did Porfirio Diaz play in the industrialization of Mexico in the last third of the nineteenth century? Was Elizabeth I's stance toward English Puritans a matter of principle or politics? At what point did public opinion in the United States swing decisively in favor of immigration restriction in the early twentieth century? But these are relatively bald, even jarring, ways to begin a conversation. A reader's response might well be: Why are you asking this? How did you choose this question? What's interesting about it? As with quotations and evidence (a matter we'll take up in chapter 11), it's important to set up your question, to put it in a framework.

There are at least two ways to do this. The first is beginning with a carefully calibrated generalization that sets the stage. I say "carefully calibrated," because a generalization that's too broad will make a reader impatient – what I call a "wide, wide world introduction" ("In this world there are many kinds of people. Some of those people are Mexicans. In the late nineteenth century, Mexico was led by a dictator named Porfirio Diaz ....") – while a generalization that's too narrow will seem, well, not like a generalization at all, but another abrupt start ("Porfirio Diaz sought a balanced approach to modernization, supporting the hacienda system even as he fostered industrial development").

Instead, what you need is something that establishes an issue, problem, or climate, a background for your question: "Mexico in the late nineteenth century was a weak but promising nation facing a dilemma. On the one hand, there was a widespread desire for industrial development, which would allow the nation to emerge from the shadow of its powerful and threatening neighbor to the north. On the other hand, that very neighbor would be critical in helping Mexico realize its goals."

The other thing you might want to do is convert your question from an interrogative to a proposition: Not "What role did Diaz play?" but something like "Diaz faced a series of difficult choices in trying to stabilize his regime," which gives some background as well as poses the question implicitly. Such strategies ease a reader into the discussion and set up your thesis, which should strike the reader as a discrete, arguable, yet compelling statement that invites curiosity about how and why it's true: "For the Mexican dictator Porfirio Diaz, the solution to the problem of Mexican industrial development was a kind of paradox: it involved emulating the United States and even inviting in North American capital, while seeking out European partnerships that would balance, and perhaps distance, Mexico from her overweening neighbor."

## Introducing the Thesis (and Motive)

Because it takes a little while to set up, a thesis almost always comes toward the end of an introduction. Ideally, it should be the penultimate sentence. Why penultimate? Because the final sentence of an introduction is a very good place to suggest the larger stakes – i.e. to hint at your motive. You may believe, for instance, that the whole issue of Mexican industrial development is interesting not only for its own sake, but as a case study of the promises and pitfalls for a particular kind of government – in this case, a dictatorship – asserting itself while grappling with more powerful nations. This may lead you to end the introduction with a sentence that reads something like, "Diaz navigated his dilemma with notable skill and energy, but the very paradox built into his leadership of the nation – a near feudal ruler trying to command a modern society into being – remained a cautionary tale long after he was deposed."

So let's see how this whole thing fits together as an intro:

> Mexico in the late nineteenth century was a weak but promising nation facing a dilemma. On the one hand, there was a widespread desire for industrial development, which would allow the nation to emerge from the shadow of its powerful and threatening neighbor to the north. On the other, that very neighbor would be critical in helping Mexico realize its goals. For the Mexican dictator Porfirio Diaz, the solution to the problem of Mexican industrial development was a kind of paradox: It involved emulating the United States and even inviting in North American capital, even as he sought out European partnerships that would balance, and perhaps distance, Mexico from her overweening neighbor. Diaz navigated his dilemma with notable skill and energy, but the very paradox built into his leadership of the nation – a near feudal ruler trying to command a modern society into being – remains a cautionary tale long after he was deposed.

Not exactly dazzling prose, but this introduction serves two purposes. One is that it lays out a reasonably clear argument that most readers will be able to understand. The other (and for the moment, more pressing one) is that it's a kind of blueprint for what should follow – some paragraphs about the state of Mexico in the nineteenth century, some others about Diaz and what he actually did, a couple more on how Diaz's efforts played out, and a conclusion on what lessons we can draw from the story.

This is an example I made up to illustrate a series of problems and choices you might make in the process of crafting an introduction. But let's move now to a real-life case from an essay I received from a student a few years ago:

> The early 1970s were a time of great social change. It was becoming fashionable to be different among much of society. In New York City, the change was hard to ignore. The gay rights movement had begun in 1969 with the Stonewall Riot, a police raid on a gay bar, and the gay community was just beginning to be accepted. *Dog Day Afternoon* [1975], directed by Sidney Lumet, was one of the first movies to portray gays in a way non-gays could

relate to. The movie supports what the gay rights movement was trying to show, that gays are people too, and their feelings, motives, and actions are the same as everyone else's.[1]

I consider this a good introduction. It lays out a question ("How does *Dog Day Afternoon* document social change?" as well as a clear thesis (the movie "was one of the first movies to portray gays in a way non-gays could relate to"). The motive does not quite have the same degree of clarity in terms of making a discrete assertion, though it's not hard to see where the author is going, largely because her diction and the construction of her sentences make clear that she's supportive of gay rights and believes the movie was an instrument as well as a document of social change (*Dog Day Afternoon* shows that "gays are people too, and their feeling, motives, and actions are the same as everyone else's").

The thing I like the most about this intro, however, is its brevity. It comes in at just over 100 words, which is about a third of a page in a typically formatted student essay. The typical reader of a student essay – a harried teacher who's reading dozens at a time – really wants a student to get to the point quickly. A concise statement of the argument is almost always going to be appreciated more than an elaborate set-up, extended metaphor, or other attempt to favor style over substance. When it comes to this kind of writing, substance *is* style.

That's not to say that some carefully considered elaboration is a bad idea. Consider the following, particularly in terms of the question side of the argument equation:

> Abraham Lincoln was not a simple man; he was not a man who could be classified easily. Though he hailed from humble, frontier birth, he would make a fortune defending America's largest corporations in court. Though he received extremely little formal education, Lincoln would become one of history's greatest political

---

[1] Kate Goldman, "Dog Day Afternoon: Realizing Our Similarities," written for Jim Cullen's "United States Since 1940" course, the Fieldston School, January 9, 2003. Essay in the collection of the author. The essayist, by the way, is the director's granddaughter.

writers. Though modern observers may be concerned by Lincoln's fairly blatant racism (he always favored colonization over integration), his contemporary opponents feared that he favored immediate equality of the races and were not above capitalizing on the populace's racist fears. Of these apparent contradictions and paradoxes the starkest are related to Lincoln's family background. Throughout his political career, Abraham Lincoln took positions that were generally unpopular among men from similar poor, frontier locations. By consistently supporting these causes which were so unpopular among the men of Kentucky and southern Illinois, where he spent most of his youth, Abraham Lincoln was a traitor to his class.[2]

Variations on the question, "What made Lincoln different?" have been asked and answered many times. And it has often been observed that he was a complex man. Indeed, such matters have been raised so often that they've become virtual clichés. In the space of a few sentences – sentences stitched together by a parallel structure of beginning with the word "though" and juxtaposing two seeming paradoxes – this writer dramatizes just what a bundle of contradictions Lincoln really was before zeroing in on what he regards as the most striking contradiction of all: that Lincoln was "a traitor to his class."

## Introducing the Key Term

Using a word like "traitor" in an essay certainly grabs a reader's attention, which is good. But – and I don't think I can emphasize this strongly enough – *you must define important words or concepts – what are sometimes called **key terms** – early on in your essay.* If you can't easily do this in the first paragraph, it may make sense to devote the second to defining your term – one of those relatively rare cases in a student essay when what constitutes an introduction might run longer than a single paragraph. A word like

---

[2]  Stephen Abrams-Downey, "Abraham Lincoln as a Traitor to His Class," written for Jim Cullen's Civil War seminar, the Fieldston School, March 2007. Essay in the collection of the author.

"traitor," which seems straightforward enough, can actually have a number of shadings: a literal, punishable crime; an immoral, though not necessarily illegal betrayal of one's comrades, ideological or otherwise; or a figurative expression that may be ironic, even approving, as it happens to be in the case of the essay in question.

Many times, the success or failure of an essay will turn on an author's awareness, or lack thereof, in defining key terms. For a number of years while teaching a modern U.S. history course, I would use a Document-Based Question, or "DBQ" (more on this in appendix D), that asked, "Was the Cold War a Product of Paranoia?" Inevitably, there were a number of essays every time with theses that said, in effect, yes, the Cold War was a product of paranoia, stemming from superpower anxiety about Mutually Assured Destruction in the age of nuclear weapons. But since paranoia is, by definition, an irrational fear (little green men are out to get me – that's paranoia) and the possibility of the world ending in a nuclear catastrophe was an all-too plausible scenario, such an argument doesn't really make any sense.

Usually an essay with a definition problem doesn't fall on its face that squarely, because, as already suggested, key terms usually have more than one meaning – they are, as they should be in analytic essays, arguable – and readers more often than not are willing to tolerate a definition that strays from the conventional understanding of a term, or even their own personal definition of a term, if they feel a writer is aware of these ambiguities and smart enough to address them. The most commonly used, and clumsy, way of doing so is with a sentence that says something like, "According to *Webster's*, the word X is defined as …". That's better than nothing. But if you can find a more graceful way of defining a term, particularly as a way of lending texture and interest to your question, the essay will get off on a much better footing. Something like, "Many people are fond of invoking, even celebrating, term Y, but many fewer are willing to elaborate on what they mean by it. Person A says it's this; person B says it's that. What's really notable about my essay subject C, though, is that for her, Y has always meant Z. That's the source of her greatness, and the basis of a vision that should be ours as well."

Problems of definition are particularly acute in the field of history, because in many cases the meanings of terms are themselves historically bound. Calling Abraham Lincoln a racist because he believed in white supremacy is certainly an accurate statement, as he is on the record multiple times as saying as much, notably in his 1858 U.S. Senate debates with Stephen Douglas. But since virtually every white American, even abolitionists, were racists by that definition, calling Lincoln one isn't a particularly useful or helpful assertion, a little like a geneticist saying 100 percent of all men have Y chromosomes. Adding an adjective – calling Lincoln an "enlightened" or "pragmatic" racist might help, because then, as now, racism took different forms, though you still have an obligation to explain what you mean, something that perhaps is most usefully done by comparing Lincoln's form of racism with that of a slaveholding Southerner or a Northern Democrat. When the definition of a term is central, as opposed to incidental, to an essayist's thesis, it may take a while to finish the process of persuasively defining a key term. But even – especially – in a case like that, the work needs to get underway early on in the essay.

## Introducing the Premise

There is one variant on the idea of the concept of a key term that needs to be mentioned here, and that is the somewhat more complex one of a *premise*. A premise is not so much a term or idea as it is a proposition. It's not quite enough of a proposition to really qualify as a thesis; rather, it's an idea that *sets up* a thesis, much in the way that a key term does. If a thesis is an assertion that's *not* obvious but true, a premise is an idea that *is* obviously true, but which needs to be said for an argument to really make sense. If it isn't said, then the idea is an assumption. Assumptions are not necessarily a problem – you can't function without them – but you don't want to avoid ones that will prevent a reader from comprehending or accepting your argument. Assuming your reader will understand English is reasonable (or, at any rate, necessary). Assuming everybody loves chocolate ice cream is not, though it may be possible to construct a reasonable premise that chocolate ice cream is a real crowd pleaser at a typical picnic.

A premise is an idea often prefaced with the word *since:* "Since the Republican Party has long been considered a champion of business interests (premise), Theodore Roosevelt's assault on monopolies from within the party made him the most important political figure of the Progressive era (thesis)." Few people would challenge the notion that Republicans typically represent business interests; more people would challenge the notion that TR was *the* most important Progressive – that's something your essay will have to demonstrate.

## Watch Your Language: Diction

Note the difference between calling Theodore Roosevelt *an* important Progressive and Theodore *the* most important Progressive. A single word, in this case the choice to use a definite article ("the") instead of an indefinite article ("an"), bears tremendous interpretive weight. Word choice – also known as diction – is always important in an essay, but nowhere is it more important than an introduction, where the parameters of an argument are first established.

Part of establishing those parameters is your tone, also an important dimension of diction. Sometimes diction is important simply in establishing your intellectual seriousness. There's a big difference between describing the twelfth-century Kurdish leader Saladin as "an impressive figure" and describing him as "a really great guy," even when neither phrase tells us all that much (*in what way* was he impressive?) The former at least suggests some respect; the latter seems to treat him like an acquaintance you like but don't know that well (or someone you neither know nor like but will say as much in order to be agreeable to the person with whom you happen to be conversing).

In still other cases, diction is important for calibrating the intensity or legitimacy of your argument. Here you want to pique a reader's interest without going overboard. Saying something like "Nelson Mandela was one of the more famous South Africans of the twentieth century" doesn't exactly make a reader's heart race. On the other hand, asserting that "Nelson Mandela was a far more important figure in the history of the world than Thomas Jefferson," is certainly striking, but not especially helpful. That's not only because such a statement is potentially polarizing in an unnecessary way (do we really have to rank famous historical figures on a vague scale of "importance?" Perhaps a more specific reference to revolution or race relations would be better?), but also because you have to wonder how meaningful a comparison between two figures living at such different times in such different contexts could ever be. That said, a striking word or phrase that pushes the envelope a bit can make a huge difference in the success of an essay. Calling Abraham Lincoln a "traitor" is a pretty serious charge, and one should be careful about even asking the question if it applies to someone. Yet in the example quoted earlier in this chapter, there's an element of irony in raising the question about someone considered one of the great heroes of American history – and not only answering it in the affirmative, but suggesting it was a good thing that Lincoln *was* a traitor to his class. The choice of the word heightens the drama and interest in the essay much more than a thesis that suggested Abraham Lincoln's political views strayed from those with whom he grew up. The right word matters. A lot.

Any discussion about key terms, premises, or diction serves as a reminder that almost as soon as we make an argument in a few words, we find ourselves drawn into the task of justifying it in a few (or more than a few) more. The site of the former is the introduction of an essay. The site of the latter, to which we will turn for the next few chapters, is the body.

# Chapter 10
# Strong Bodies (I):
# The Work of Topic Sentences

- Inter- and intra-paragraph organization
- Directing topic sentence traffic: double signposts
- Clues for the clueless: breaking down the thesis
- Don't stick with the facts

Like a lot of complex organisms, an essay is a series of interlocking pieces made up of smaller units. Letters make words; words make sentences; sentences make paragraphs. Paragraphs are a crucial component in the construction of an essay, and they're the one readers are most likely to be conscious of as they read. Arguments are the DNA, and in a good one they thread through the whole essay, right down to which word is chosen. But paragraphs are the organs, the most visible parts of an essay that do the work of embodying the argument and keeping the rest of it alive.

Paragraphs are also worlds in themselves. In a well-written essay, each one has a discrete job to do. And each one has discrete components of its own. The most important is the *topic sentence*, which organizes a paragraph by informing a reader of its focus. Paragraphs are also the main repository for *evidence* and *counter-evidence*, drawn from the sources that are the life-blood of an essay (especially a history essay). But evidence, however vital, never stands alone. And so good paragraphs also provide *exposition*, a writer's own words that set up, explain, and connect the various kinds of evidence that come from those sources. We'll have more to say about that in the next two chapters. Most of my focus here will be on topic sentences, which act like the hormones of a paragraph that regulate the relationship between the internal logic of an essay and the outside world of its readers. When the various levels are in synch and interacting well, an essay hums along. When they aren't, the essay might still function, but its rhythms are off, a reader can get lost, and a break in logic, attention, or credibility can result.

Most of the principal work of good paragraphing takes place in the body of an essay. To be sure, introductions and conclusions – what I call the *frame* (more on this in chapter 14) – are composed of paragraphs, sometimes multiple ones. But frames are typically about conceptualizing an argument, and bodies are typically about elaborating upon and supporting that argument. Bodies do the heavy lifting, and paragraphs provide the muscle. Just as important, paragraphs act in coordination. Introductions can stand alone. Indeed, in chapter 9, I could present them without any effort to include the rest of an essay and still have them make perfect sense to you. But while a paragraph can and does function as an autonomous unit, its value very often depends not only on how it does its job, but how it relates to other paragraphs (and how well they do *their* jobs). Body paragraphs are natural communitarians.

## Inter- and Intra-paragraph Organization

Indeed, when a teacher speaks of a "well-organized essay," it's quite likely that, perhaps not even realizing it, she's referring to two discrete phenomena: *inter*-paragraph organization and *intra*-paragraph organization. I use the term intra-paragraph organization to describe how coherent a particular paragraph is on its own terms – whether the topic sentence is clear; whether the various sentences that make up a paragraph flow; whether the sources that are quoted or cited make sense or are used appropriately. Take this paragraph from the body of a U.S. history essay:

> Student protest and unrest ultimately culminated in societal change.
> For example, during the fall of 1964 [the University of California
> at] Berkeley declared that "non-campus political literature could

no longer be distributed on the Berkeley campus." The new rule seemed to be a violation of the inherent right to open political discussion. Led by Mario Savio, a veteran of Freedom Summer in Mississippi, students responded with massive protests and the Free Speech Movement was born. Savio declared that institutions of higher education had become "odious machines which treated students like objects." He urged students to "put their bodies against the gears, against the wheels – and make the machine stop until we are free."[1]

This is a healthy body paragraph with good intra-paragraph organization. It begins with a topic sentence that's pleasingly concise, easy to digest, and one that indicates just what the rest of the paragraph is going to be about. The author then jumps immediately to supporting her point, which she signals with the words "for example." She makes an aside with a clause that describes Mario Savio as "a veteran of Freedom Summer in Mississippi," a truly useful detail, since Freedom Summer was another example of student protest and makes clear that the Free Speech Movement was not an isolated incident (and that Savio was part of something much larger than a school protest). This particular paragraph happens to be contextual; it comes fairly early in a piece that focuses on the work of counterculture writer Ken Kesey. So it has a place in a larger story even as it stands on its own.

Actually, the very best paragraphs are governed by topic sentences that are not only internally coherent, but are also aligned with those that proceed and follow – that are marked by strong inter-paragraph organization. The simplest application of this idea is one you see all the time, where a writer will discuss a string of related ideas or examples. Then one paragraph will begin with a sentence like "The first manifestation of W emerged during the

---

[1]  Kate Pier, "Ken Kesey's Mental Institution: A Microcosm of the Radical Counterculture in the United States," written for Jim Cullen's "U.S. Since 1940" class, the Fieldston School, January 12, 2003. Essay in the collection of the author. For the sake of clarity, I did not include the author's footnotes, which followed the quotes from the unnamed Berkeley official and Savio. Both came from William H. Chafe, *The Unfinished Journey: American Since World War II* (New York: Oxford University Press, 1999), 323.

X period, when Y did Z." Then the next paragraph begins "The second manifestation of X occurred," or "Another manifestation of X occurred," and so on. This isn't exactly thrilling prose, but it gets the job done.

## Directing Topic Sentence Traffic: Double Signposts

Words like "second" or "another" are sometimes called "double signposts": they both look ahead as well as back. A "second" implies a first, which serves to remind a reader of what's just been said. But when placed in a topic sentence, "second" also points toward where the reader is headed, i.e. the next illustration of the larger point. In the previous example, repeating the word "manifestation" does similar work of connection. Double signposts and intentional repetition are both examples of "stitching," and are important to the revision process (see chapter 14). They are extremely valuable tools. They not only help guide a reader through an essay, but can help guide a writer, too.

Indeed, topic sentences are often highly useful in the early stages of writing an essay, because they can function as an outline, marking the walls of the house long before it actually gets furnished. Much in the way that formulating the discrete components of your argument gives you the core of your introduction, so too can formulating a series of topic sentences give you the core of your body. Juxtaposing them against each other can also assist you in crafting double signposts that will stitch it together.

Topic sentences have special significance for the thesis piece of an argument. Questions can usually be unveiled in their entirety in an introduction. Motives, which can be hinted at in the introduction as well as the body (we'll talk more about that in a moment) are usually based in the conclusion. But the thesis, which is the heart of an argument, finds its home in the body of an essay. To a great degree, that's because unlike the question or the motive, the thesis involves sustained explanation that requires multiple paragraphs. Since, as I've already suggested, a thesis is an assertion that's not obvious, but true, then it's going to take a little doing to *make* it obvious. This typically involves breaking the thesis down into a series of steps or components – if you *can't* break your thesis down into parts or examples, it's time to start thinking about a new thesis. Each of those components should be assigned a topic sentence.

## Clues for the Clueless: Breaking Down the Thesis

When you're reading a really good essay, you can make sense of what an author is doing on the basis of the topic sentences alone. I used to assign an essay that asked students to make a historical comparison between the protagonist of Jane Austen's 1816 novel *Emma* and her reimagined twentieth-century counterpart, Cher Horowitz (Alicia Silverstone), in writer/director Amy Heckerling's 1995 film *Clueless*. Here's a string of topic sentences from one essay I received:

> "Although Heckerling relocates the story from the 19th-century English countryside to a modern-day Los Angeles high school, Cher and Emma stand on the same rung of the social ladder."

> "Because of Emma and Cher's social seclusion, both end up spoiled by their situations in life."

> "The snobbery that Emma and Cher demonstrate eventually results in painful humiliation that prompts their moral progress."[2]

Each of these sentences supports a paragraph that includes quotes, analysis, and other forms of evidence. But they almost read like they could be part of a single paragraph on their own. What's particularly nice about these sentences is the way they trace a narrative arc – the writer moves *through* the movie, and yet it's not the storyline that shapes the essay, but her own analysis.

---

[2]  Liane Lee Young, "Parallel Lives, Parallel Lessons in Highbury and Hollywood," an essay written for Jim Cullen's "The Culture of Schools" class at Harvard University, December 5, 2000. Essay in the collection of the author.

At the core of that analysis is a thesis that asserts these two seemingly different characters are very much alike.

It's important to note that strong topic sentences transcend their content. Here's another essay from the same assignment that makes the opposite argument: that it's the historical differences, not superficial similarities, which define the two people most vividly:

> "Emma and Cher both have problems in deluding themselves about how people feel about them."

> "Yet the noticeable similarities regarding their obliviousness toward others' loving them (or not loving them) is less important than the differences between the characters."

> "Their difference in handling love mishaps illustrates a change in society's outlook on adolescent women."[3]

Here the writer takes a paragraph to note that the two females do have their similarities. But through the crucial deployment of the word "yet" in the second topic sentence, he goes on to explain that such similarities are superficial, not only because the stories play out in different ways (Cher's love interest is a homosexual, for example, a scenario that would never ever be broached in an early nineteenth-century novel), but more importantly because the outcome of the story reveals the impact of modern feminism – a movement prominent both in Britain and the United States – in shaping societies expectations and parameters for women.

There are a couple of additional lessons to be drawn from looking at these sets of topic sentences, both rooted in the nature of this particular assignment, which is, like so many assignments in History and other subjects, *comparative* in nature. The first is that any thesis you hope to advance should always be conducted with at least an awareness of alternatives, and that awareness

---

[3]  Mark Tortorella, "Superficially Similar: Character and Societal Views," written for Jim Cullen's "The Culture of Schools" class, Harvard University, April 9, 2001. Essay in the collection of the author.

should be regularly conveyed in your topic sentences. It's *because* Emma and Cher seem so different that their *similarities* are so important. Or, conversely, it's *because* Emma and Cher seem so alike that their *differences* are so important. (To say they're alike because they both live in big houses, or different because one's name is four letters long and the other is five letters long is to say things that are true, but meaningless.) I'll have more to say on how to deal with positions contrary to the one you want to take in chapter 12.

The second important point about comparative essays is that you always want your ideas, not those of your sources, to drive your topic sentences. In the examples above, the writers use the plot of a novel, but their arguments are not defined by it. Moreover, they skillfully juggle the two characters within one idea in all their topic sentences. A less sophisticated writer might spend a few paragraphs on Emma and then another few on Cher, and, strictly speaking, there's nothing wrong with that. But an essay has a lot more analytic energy, and thus interest, when the ideas, rather than characters or events, are driving it forward.

## Don't Stick With the Facts

Whatever you do, *never use a topic sentence for merely factual purposes*. A sentence that merely says something like, "On November 11, 1918, the First World War finally ended," unless you're immediately going to follow up with an analytic statement that explains why such a fact is relevant or useful. A writer whose work consists of a series of facts or dates isn't writing an essay at all, but a report. And academically speaking, you're beyond that now.

I should point out that in essays, as in many other enterprises, rules are made to be broken (though they're best broken by people who know how to play by them in the first place). All the examples I've used in this chapter have topic sentences at the beginning of the paragraph. But while that's a good rule of thumb for reading as well as writing, there are justifiable variations. This is particularly true in the case of texts that do not conform to the typical norms of academic history, though confident and agile scholars can also tweak established conventions to good effect. Take, for example, this discussion of Herbert Hoover's presidency, from Richard Hoftstadter's much-celebrated *The American Political Tradition*. Hoover, Hofstadter is explaining, lacked the psychological resources to confront the Great Depression because by temperament and training he looked backward rather than forward. He's just finished a discussion of Hoover's economic philosophy, and then shifts to another aspect of his background:

> Hoover, moreover, was trained as an engineer, and his social philosophy was infected with professional bias. Economy and efficiency became ends in themselves. To him it mattered dearly not only what goals were adopted but exactly how a job was done. This craftsmanlike concern for technique, a legitimate thing in itself, stood him in bad stead politically during the depression, when people grew impatient for results rather than method.[4]

Here, the topic sentence ("Economy and efficiency became ends in themselves") comes second rather than first. Hoftstadter uses that first slot to bind his discussion of the last paragraph on Hoover's economics background with that of his engineering background, cemented by the double signpost of "moreover." He can get away with this because the topic sentence follows quickly, and when it does it's notable for its economy and clarity.

There's one other thing worth noting in this paragraph, which is the way that Hoftstadter is not only advancing his thesis here (about Hoover's psychological, even more than ideological, conservatism), but also a motive. He's explaining why Hoover reacted the way he did, but he's also conveying a sense of disapproval, a *stance* toward what he's describing. A word like "infected" suggests Hoover's intellectual profile was diseased. And following it in the topic sentence by saying his preoccupation with economy and efficiency became ends in themselves makes his approach to national problems seem cramped and misguided. The very best

[4] Richard Hofstadter, *The American Political Tradition and the Men Who Made It* (1948; New York: Vintage, 1962), 296.

96

writers will give flavor to their prose, particularly topic sentences, through diction that signals their feelings even as they convey their ideas.

No matter how cogent or lively a writer's prose is, however, a persuasive argument is finally going to rest on the sources a writer uses. The *way* a historian uses those sources – the facts, logic, inferences, and other manipulations of documents she incorporates into her work – falls into the realm of our next topic of discussion: evidence.

# Chapter 11

# Strong Bodies (II): Exposition and Evidence

- Too much of a good thing: using quotations selectively
- Seeing is not necessarily believing
- Beware of "negroes" and "Orientals"
- Lies, damn lies, and statistics

By now, I'm sure you understand that real History never stands alone. Arresting ideas and clear organization are vitally important, but a good piece of historical writing – which is to say a persuasive piece of historical writing – is only as good as its sources. What counts as sufficient and credible in the realm of sources is going to vary from reader to reader, and, perhaps more decisively, by the quality and quantity of what's available to you in any particular project. I can't help you much with that. But the *way* you work with what you've got is something that merits some discussion.

The various ways you perform that work – the choices you make in *which* sources you use, how *much* of those sources you use, the *sequence* in which you use them – falls into the realm of exposition. It's all fine and good to have a good thesis in the introduction of an essay, and to have strong topic sentences in the body. An essay can't be good without them. But if that's *all* you've got, if the essay consists of nothing more than a string of assertions unsupported with facts, context, evidence, and other kinds of information that help explain what you're trying to say, that essay will seem thin and unconvincing. Exposition is the tissue, the muscle, of all good writing. Without it an essay will wobble and fall down. It needs exposition, and it needs that exposition to be executed with some care.

One of the most obvious ways in which this lack of expository muscle tone manifests itself is in the way students quote their sources. Every time I assign an essay, I'll get work that never fails to surprise me in the awkwardness (laziness?) with which some students quote their sources. I'll protect the non-innocent by not citing real-life examples, but the following comes close enough for you to get my point. Let's say you're writing an essay for a women's history course on the evolution of schooling for girls in nineteenth-century Europe – we'll call it something like "Of Two Minds: The Quest for Equity in Women's Education in the Victorian Era." Having done your literal and figurative home-work, you're aware that the English writer Mary Wollstonecraft wrote a 1792 treatise, *A Vindication of the Rights of Woman*, that you deem relevant background to your argument. And so you craft a paragraph early in the body of the essay to quote this primary source:

> The roots of the quest for gender equity in education go back at least as far as the 1700s. "If women are not a swarm of ephemeron triflers, why should they be kept in ignorance under the specious name of innocence?" By the mid-nineteenth century, efforts to begin female academies –....

There are still all kinds of things missing here, even if we make the dubious assumption that this hypothetical writer provided a footnote for the quote (which I will momentarily). A reader still needs to know, right then and there, who's speaking in what source at what time. That reader also needs to know who Mary Wollstonecraft was – it may well be that she's a familiar figure, whether because she's been extensively discussed in class, or because this is an advanced course, and Wollstonecraft would be well known as one of the founding mothers of feminism. But she still needs a tag, a label, that explains why she's showing up in this particular essay. In effect, we need to be told *which* Mary Wollstonecraft is being paged: the working woman who overcame severe personal setbacks? The contemporary of leading intellectuals like Thomas Paine and William Blake? Or some other Mary Wollstonecraft? Finally, there should be some analytic *use* of a source you deemed worthy to quote. This particular one happens to be a (rhetorical) question. What's the context for that question? What do we know, or can we infer, of Wollstonecraft's answer?

In short, *any quotation you use in an essay must be set up, identified, and followed through.* Let's try again:

> The roots of the quest for gender equity in education go back at least as far as the 1700s. Mary Wollstonecraft, whose famous 1792 manifesto *A Vindication of the Rights of Women* focused specifically on this question, noted that many male writers assumed that women were not capable of virtue. Yet, she noted, God endowed them with souls no less than those of men, prompting her to ask the rhetorical question, "If women are not a swarm of ephemeron triflers, why should they be kept in ignorance under the specious name of innocence?"[1] By the mid-nineteenth century, many women, and even a few men, were asking the same question. Early efforts to address it took the form of ....

Here, I hope you'll agree, is a writer with much more control of the material. And this really is the point: it's about other people being used in the service of your ideas. But you need to respect those other people, and give them and their work the credit and consideration they deserve, not only in identifying them, but in putting their work into an appropriate perspective.

## Too Much of a Good Thing: Using Quotations Selectively

So far, I've been talking about sins of omission. But I often see the opposite kind, too, of an essayist giving a reader far too much rather than far too little. Sometimes that's because a writer is too

---

[1] Mary Wollstonecraft, *A Vindication of the Rights of Woman* (1792; New York: Dover, 1996), 18.

lazy or diffident to actually edit a source. You never want to mis-represent what a source is saying, but that doesn't mean you have to quote it verbatim. Let's say, for example, that you're writing about the famous Funeral Oration of Pericles, and want to focus on how he's trying to motivate the Athenians of the fifth century BCE, at the beginning of the Peloponnesian War. You know enough not to quote the whole thing (as recorded by Thucydides), but nevertheless provide your reader with the following:

> So died these men as became Athenians. You, their survivors, must determine to have as unfaltering a resolution in the field, though you may pray that it may have a happier issue. And not contented with ideas derived only from words of the advantages which are bound up with the defence of your country, though these would furnish a valuable text to a speaker even before an audience so alive to them as the present, you must yourselves realize the power of Athens, and feed your eyes upon her from day to day, till love of her fills your hearts; and then, when all her greatness shall break upon you, you must reflect that it was by courage, sense of duty, and a keen feeling of honour in action that men were enabled to win all this, and that no personal failure in an enterprise could make them consent to deprive their country of their valour, but they laid it at her feet as the most glorious contribution that they could offer.[2]

Pericles' Funeral Oration is a masterpiece of world literature that can hardly be improved by anyone's attempt to rewrite it. But if your purpose is to point out the underlying strategy of his death-less prose, you may not need to quote all that much. You can simply say, "Pericles told his fellow Athenians that they must honor their fallen comrade not only with words, but also with deeds." If there is a particular phrase or collection of phrases that you find colorful or useful, could simply highlight them: Pericles called for "unfaltering resolution," reminding Athenians that "you must

---

[2] Thucydides, *History of the Peloponnesian War*, translated by Richard Crawley. Available at the Massachusetts Institute of Technology's Internet Access Archive: http://classics.mit.edu/Thucydides/pelopwar.2.second.html (accessed July 15, 2007).

yourselves realize the power of Athens, and feed your eyes upon her from day to day, till love of her fills your hearts." Feel free to break up and edit quotes for the sake of flow in a sentence, or to highlight words or phrases that you consider important:

> Cullen told his reader to "feel free" to "highlight" key words.

> "Feel free ... to highlight words or phrases," Cullen advised.

Of course, there may be situations where you think you want to quote a big chunk of a document, the way I have above. I will warn you, however, that I regard such block quotes as guilty until proven innocent. I don't deny that they have their place, and that they may be particularly useful in the research or early drafting stage, when you're trying to sort through and structure your material. But sooner or later you need to chisel most of them down, because no matter how worthy they are, many readers are going to jump right over them. (You didn't actually read that whole excerpt of the Funeral Oration, did you?)

There are strategies you can use to keep your reader engaged with a big excerpt from a source. One is to preface the quotation by saying something like, "Because he speaks with such grace and insight, it is worth quoting Pericles at some length." Better still is to tell your reader in advance just what to be looking for: "Note how, in the following passage, Pericles consistently emphasizes an instrumental approach to memory – that honoring the dead is an active process." And of course, you can keep your reader on track, or even looking back, by coming out of the quote by either analyzing what you've just quoted, or making clear that it's crucial for understanding what comes next: "Pericles' injunction to his countrymen would only become more urgent in the coming years, as a dreadful plague and military setbacks challenged Athenian confidence."

## Seeing is Not Necessarily Believing

However much or however little you quote a source, you should be confident it will be likely to bolster the position you're taking.

The first and perhaps most important point to keep in mind is that somebody saying something doesn't necessarily make it so. A source may be speaking before the outcome of an event was known. Or a source may have a perspective that's limited. Or, simply, a source may be lying. Seeing should not be the same as believing: The Chinese government produced films in the 1950s depicting happy workers making tremendous strides in agricultural productivity at a time when millions were starving. Even statements that are likely to be true must sometimes be taken with a grain of salt. In leafing through *Life* Magazine from March 16, 1942, when U.S. involvement in World War II was fully engaged, and citizens at home were fully mobilized, you will come across a statement that reads, "Illness, contagion must not be permitted to slacken our speed – or weaken the staggering blow our nation has set itself to deliver." Given that this statement comes from an advertisement for Dixie, a paper-cup company seeking to benefit financially from concerns about spreading microbes, it would be unwise simply to accept it at face value. The statement may well be true, and you can certainly use it, but it's best that you note the source and try to reinforce it with similar assertions from other perspectives, like a quote from a government official, or a memoir written years later that discusses such efforts.

Such considerations are especially important to keep in mind when using primary sources. They often require context, and context often requires you to have done enough background research to provide it. But some of the same issues can arise when using secondary sources as well. "A western democracy has been born in the land of the Prophets, but the backlash of a feudal past still seeks to block recognition of the forces of progress that Israel has brought to the Middle East," concludes a study of Middle Eastern politics published in 1973, the year in which an Arab–Israeli war took place.[3] Many people then and now would agree with this assessment. But given that it appears in a book with the title *And the Hills Shouted for Joy: The Day Israel Was Born*, one should

[3] Bernard Postal and Henry W. Levy, *And the Hills Shouted for Joy: The Day Israel Was Born* (New York: David McKay Company, 1973), 387.

103

also consider the possibility that to an Egyptian or a Palestinian, it might not have been joy that the hills were shouting for.

## Beware of "Negroes" and "Orientals"

You should also keep in mind that Histories themselves get dated, and a scholarly study that might be considered authoritative in one period may not remain so forever. This is particularly true in the area of race relations. "The American negroes are the only people in the world, as far as I know, that ever became free without any effort of their own," opined a biographer of Civil War general Ulysses S. Grant in a biography published decades after his death. "They twanged banjos around the railroad stations, sang melodious spirituals, and believed some Yankee would soon come along and give each of them forty acres and a mule."[4] Most of us would recognize this as an outrageously racist statement – one actively refuted by subsequent generations of scholars. One cue we have of its outmoded character is the author's use of the word "negro," as opposed to "black" (increasingly favored in the 1960s), or "Afro-American" (adopted by some in the 1970s), or African American (the term of choice at the turn of this century, without the hyphen, since "African-American" recalls for some the term "hyphenated American" of a century ago, to suggest that people like Italian-Americans or Polish-Americans weren't quite fully one of us).

Sometimes the indication that a work may not reflect contemporary understanding of a topic is more subtle. No reputable publisher today would publish a book that the once highly reputable Liveright Corporation did in multiple editions with a title like *The Story of the American Indian*.[5] Besides the fact that many people (though not all Indians themselves) prefer the term "Native American," a notion there is *the* story would itself be questioned

---

[4] Remark by biographer W. E. Woodward cited in Jim Cullen, *The Civil War in Popular Culture: A Reusable Past* (Washington D.C.: Smithsonian Institution Press, 1995), 145.

[5] Paul Radin, *The Story of the American Indian* (1927; New York: Liveright, 1944).

if not outright rejected. Lumping together a highly variegated group of people this way, like "Asiatics" (a term which, like "Orientals" was once common) or even "gringos," is not really considered appropriate in scholarly circles, even if some people do so informally or to make a political point. Newer scholarship is not necessarily better scholarship, though before you actually cite a secondary source that's more than, say, 30 years old, it's worth checking to see whether its conclusions are still considered valid. This is where a tertiary source like *The Encyclopedia of North American Indians*, for example, might be helpful.[6]

## Lies, Damn Lies, and Statistics

One kind of source we haven't discussed much, in large measure because it's a world unto itself, are quantitative sources. But we need to at least touch on them, because in the immortal words that were not quite Mark Twain's, "There are lies, damn lies, and statistics."[7] You should exercise care in your use of data even if you assume it's accurate, because it's still easy to confuse or mislead a reader. If, for example, you compare rates of voter participation in two countries, but in one case the information is based on registered voters and the other it's based on total population, you're going to be presenting a misleading picture. Financial data is particularly tricky, especially in History, because it's often extremely difficult to ascertain what an English pound was worth in 1810, or how much a 1790 dollar would buy in 1960 (though if you're going to trust anybody on this, it would be a historian who seems to show real comfort and authority with this kind of conversion and an explanation somewhere in the book about

[6] *The Encyclopedia of North American Indians,* edited by Frederick Hoxie (Boston: Houghton Mifflin,1996).
[7] According to Roger Rees, whose BBC radio show and website have become a kind of national institution in Britain, Twain's remark was published posthumously and attributed to the nineteenth-century British Prime Minister Benjamin Disraeli. Rees notes, however, that the comment has not been successfully traced to Disraeli. See http://www1c.btwebworld.com/quote-unquote/p0000149.htm (accessed July 16, 2007).

how such calculations are being made). In the kind of expository essays we're talking about here, it's best to be highly discriminating in numbers that you use, and to be selective in citing them, not only because they're likely to be contested, but because there's only so much statistical data a reader can absorb in a document whose primary thrust is likely to be rhetorical rather than quantitative.

You may at this point be feeling a bit daunted, if not irritated: With so many considerations, and so many pitfalls, using evidence might begin to seem like more trouble than it's worth. Let me remind you, then, that writing an essay is a matter of *essaying*, of trying out. Go ahead and say/quote what you believe to be true. No one is going to sue you for anything you say in an academic essay. Nor are you expected to prove anything to anybody. Yes, you probably are being graded by a fallible human being whose assessment of you may well be different than that of another fallible human being. To a great extent, that grade will be determined on the basis of your demonstration of particular skills, like being able to articulate and structure an argument. But you're also being graded on your *judgment*, on the choices you make in terms of what you think matters, in what you include in an essay and what you don't. If you go about this in a thoughtful way – and, really, this is at least half the battle – a growing percentage of fallible human beings who grade you will say, in so many words, "nice job." And as you know, academic success is to a great degree a matter of percentages.

Part of what "nice job" means is, "You show real confidence and skill in expressing yourself." But that, in turn, is a reflection of your confidence and skill in paying attention not only to what other people think, but in anticipating what they're *likely* to think before you've even finished writing an essay. And this brings us back to the issue of evidence again – or, more accurately counter-evidence, and the related skill of counter-argument. We need to spend some time considering that.

# Chapter 12

# Strong Bodies (III): Counterargument and Counterevidence

- Two sides to every story – at a minimum
- Don't condescend
- Show, don't tell

When Chandra Manning went to a friend's wedding in 2005, she did not intend to be drawn into an intense discussion of the Civil War. The young scholar (by which I mean she was about thirty; compared with economists and tennis players, historians tend to develop slowly and peak late) had been working for years on a doctoral dissertation, soon to become her first book, on Civil War soldiers and their attitudes toward slavery. But the man she met from Buffalo did not know this, and she did not tell him. What he told her, over the course of an hour-long conversation, was that slavery had nothing to do with the conflict. Reflecting later on their exchange, and on the intensity of his opinion, Manning mused, "Who can blame him?" After all, she noted, most soldiers who fought for the Confederacy had no slaves, and few Union soldiers had ever laid eyes on one, much less expressed a desire to wage a war of racial liberation. Indeed, most white people, North and South, were avowed racists. So it seems hard to say African Americans were what the fight was all about.

Manning knew that the opinions of the man from Buffalo were not unique. Actually, her book, *What this Cruel War Was Over*, is an extended reply to such people. The main body of her evidence consists of writings from 657 Union soldiers and 477 Confederates, spread over 45 states and two countries, along with about a hundred regimental newspapers. From a detailed examination of these and other records, Manning concluded that slavery lay at the very heart at the combatants' thoughts and feelings. As she and other historians (myself among them) have noted, there is a kind of culture gap between academic historians, who tend to view slavery as central to the cause and meaning of the war, and the public at large, which tends not to agree. Manning hoped to close that gap with a fresh set of detailed evidence that addressed the debate directly.[1]

But Manning's book was not only a response to people like that Civil War buff from Buffalo (who, in my experience, are far more likely to be instinctively skeptical of a Harvard Ph.D. like Manning than be persuaded by her). She was also addressing her peers inside the profession. In the introduction of her book she notes that a number of recent historians, among them James McPherson (who I discuss in chapter 6) have explored the attitudes of ordinary Civil War soldiers. But, she notes, most previous studies have lumped them together, not distinguishing between Union and Confederate perspectives – or the evolution of such perspectives over time. She also gives an unusual degree of prominence to the views African American soldiers, who, she argues, had a distinct view of the war of their own.

In short, *What this Cruel War Was Over* is a book that in many ways was conceived as a self-conscious response to readers with whom Chandra Manning disagrees. While in fact many scholarly books and articles have similar objectives, hers is a very good example of what might be considered a work of history premised on *counterargument*, as a piece of work that seeks to engage, and change, the tenor of an existing debate. If a work is dedicated

---

[1] Chandra Manning, *What this Cruel War Was Over: Soldiers, Slavery, and the Civil War* (New York: Knopf, 2007), 3–10. I examine the culture gap between academic historians and Civil War buffs in my discussion of Civil War reenactors in *The Civil War in Popular Culture: A Reusable Past* (Washington D.C.: Smithsonian Institution Press, 1995), 196–7.

to overturning or refuting a predominant point of view in such a debate, some may call that work, as I would call Manning's book, a *revisionist* work of history.

## Two Sides to Every Story – At a Minimum

Counterargument (and, to a lesser degree, revisionism) are an integral part of historical discourse. A scholar can't really achieve a national or international reputation unless she demonstrates both mastery of a topic and the ability to make an original contribution to that topic. This is a tall order – taller than most students are willing to even contemplate, much less undertake. But counterargument is nevertheless a vital and attainable skill that you should add to your bag of tricks when you write an essay.

That's because some essays you'll be assigned will ask you to weigh in on controversial topics, and you may find yourself taking what you understand to be a minority view in a debate. In such a situation, it's essential that you convey that you understand the tenor of such a debate, how people on the other side – or *sides*, because there are often more than two – of the issue think, and why you nevertheless disagree. Very often, you'll need to do so at the outset, as in this example:

> For anyone who lived through it, the Cold War can understandably be viewed as the most frightening period in the history of the world. For the first time, through the doctrine of Mutually Assured Destruction (MAD), the United States and the Soviet Union could wipe out human life in an instant through nuclear weapons. Moreover, incidents such as the Cuban Missile Crisis of 1962 showed how plausible such a scenario was, even when both sides were trying to avoid it. Paradoxically, however, the very terror MAD imposed also created long-term conditions for lasting peace: War between the superpowers became too dreadful to allow. Even more surprising, in the long-term, the U.S. strategy of calculated deterrence resulted not in an endless deadlock, but decisive victory as the Soviet Union ultimately crumbled. Such facts

bear examination for what they show us not only about the Cold War, but about challenges the United States may face in foreign policy in the 21st century.[2]

Counterargument lies at the very heart of this essay-in-the-making. The author establishes the prevailing view as concisely as possible, as well as the reasons for it (like the Cuban Missile Crisis, which as anybody who's studied it knows, was scary as hell). And yet it's abundantly clear that this essay is going to go in a very different direction. Its thesis, in effect, is that MAD was, however painful, instrumental in keeping the Cold War from ever getting too hot. The author also indicates that the body is going to explain why ("such facts bear examination"). There are also hints here of a motive, too: though the doctrine of MAD is now a part of history, it retains ongoing relevance for understanding contemporary U.S. foreign policy. An attentive reader will be curious to see not only just how this writer is going to finesse the Cuban Missile Crisis (is it really possible to suggest that fallible human beings almost blowing up the planet was really a good thing?), but how MAD can be a useful guide today. Such questions move beyond the realm of counterargument into counterevidence, something I'll address momentarily.

First, though, I want to point out that counterargument is not just something that gets articulated in the introduction. To be sure, it typically has a home there, especially in essays that are self-consciously revisionist. But counterargument threads through the body of the essay as well. Sometimes a writer will give a sentence, a paragraph or more to an alternative view, signaling a concession or acknowledgment with words like "It is true that ...." or "While it's certainly the case that ...". But then a writer will follow up with a topic sentence that begins with words like "Still,"

---

[2] Though modified, the argument here is based on Cameron Sinsenheimer's essay "How I Learned to Stop Worrying and Love the Bomb," written for Jim Cullen's "U.S. History Since 1940" class, the Fieldston School, September 2006. Essay in the author's collection. His title, by the way, is a (revisionist) allusion to Stanley Kubrick's 1964 film *Dr. Strangelove*.

or "Nevertheless" or "Yet" to signal that the argument is going to be taking a very different direction.

## Don't Condescend

In the process of crafting such exchanges, it's important not to trivialize alternative views. Phrases like "Our so-called patriotic friends would have us believe" or "Less informed observers have asserted" make you look worse than the people you describe. Give people and ideas the benefit of the doubt. History is not a winner-take-all game. You don't have to insist on every single point in an argument in order to be persuasive. Indeed, you may be all the more persuasive when you concede that your own positions are not infallible. Admit the costs of the views you hold, literal and figurative. Just be sure you also indicate your willingness to pay those costs – and why others should, too.

Indeed, one of the best student essays I've ever read involved a ten-page analysis of *Ex Parte McCardle*, a Supreme Court case which documented the excesses of Radical Republicans in the post-Civil War era of Reconstruction, who sought to limit free speech and aggrandize their own power in the name of protecting African Americans (some of these Republicans were sincere in this regard, and some were not). Such efforts were resisted by President Andrew Johnson, long a controversial figure among historians but one who in recent times has been generally regarded as misguided at best in his approach to race relations. The writer of this essay had little doubt that these Republicans were legally in the wrong in the McCardle case, which she views as symbolic of Reconstruction as a whole. And yet this is how she concludes the essay:

> However, regardless of how unjust Reconstruction was, it was always better than the alternative; it was the final attempt at establishing equality, the only one that made any impact. Herein lies the true tragedy – not what happened to William McCardle, or to Johnson's power, but that it was necessary. Without the Reconstruction Acts, blacks in the South would not have enjoyed

111

anything resembling freedom. Reconstruction disregarded many of the ideals on which the United States was founded. It was necessary, though, to fully eradicate something else on which the country had been built: slavery.[3]

One could well be troubled, even frightened, by the implications of this essay, which implies that there is a higher law of morality (whose?) that transcends mere legal questions. But one could not credibly assert in finishing this essay that the writer is not aware of the excesses and dangers in the actions of the people she ultimately chooses to defend (that's why she uses the phrase "true tragedy" to summarize her view of the case). I've said repeatedly that the goal of a good essay is to persuade a reader. But one can still fail on that basis and do something important if it provokes a reader to question or clarify his own beliefs, and think more about how (if?) they can be internally affirmed.

## Show, Don't Tell

It is never enough to simply *tell* a reader what to think, however. A good writer must also *show* why he thinks the way he does, not only by using the relevant evidence at hand, but also by acknowledging counterevidence that may contradict that view. Here's a response to the question as to how the Socialist union leader and presidential candidate Eugene Debs, who died in 1926, would feel if he visited the United States today. This student believes Debs would feel pretty good:

> The 20th century saw a rise in living conditions for the general public, including women and children. From 1900–1999 the percentage of women working rose 41% and the percentage of female lawyers rose from 1% to 28%. In 1938, as part of the Fair Labor Standards Act (a section of the New Deal), child labor was criminalized. In 1900 the per capita income (in 1999 dollars) was $4,200

[3] Hillary Aidun, "Caution: Reconstruction Ahead," written for Jim Cullen's U.S. History Survey, the Fieldston School, June 2006. Essay in the author's collection.

and the hourly production wage was $3.80, but by 1999 per capita reached $33,700 and the hourly production wage was $13.90 ....
Economic opportunity, education, and working-class rights have increased so dramatically that one wonders whether Debs would even recognize the country.

   This is not to say, of course, that many of the things Eugene Debs was fighting for have disappeared. The wealth divide in America is still high. We have a war going on that (like World War I) was begun by the elite but is being fought by the poor. The Patriot Act resembles the Sedition and Espionage Acts of 1917–18 in its repression of civil liberties ...."[4]

It's clear this writer recognizes that there are two sides to the question he's being asked – as well he should, since if there weren't it wouldn't be much of a question. But his own views are clear, supported by a barrage of statistics that convey absolute as well as relative improvement in workers' lives. This sense of material improvement – the *kind* of (economic) evidence he cites to support his view – trumps the political and legal problems that he acknowledges mar contemporary U.S. society. Another writer may well view those political and legal problems as more, well, problematic. Which is precisely the point: for a reader to get a clearly defined point of view, and come to her own conclusions.

   Sometimes the issue with evidence is not that there are contrary pieces of data, but that a particular piece of data is highly ambiguous – it can be evidence *or* counterevidence, depending on how a writer uses it. What did the reputed man called Jesus Christ mean when he allegedly said in the first century CE, "And I say unto you, it is easier for a man to pass through the eye of a needle than for one who is rich to enter the kingdom of God" (Matthew 19:24)? Should Christians, then and now, conclude that since camels cannot in fact fit through needles – any "needle" a camel *could* fit through would have to be upside down and more like a gigantic spike – rich folks are not going to heaven? Or is Jesus, who by reputation spoke cryptically and liked to confound the common sense of the time, suggesting that there are things

[4]   Jeffrey Stein, short essay on Eugene Debs, written for Jim Cullen's U.S. History Survey, the Fieldston School, February, 2007. Essay in the author's collection.

that are possible for God that are not possible for mere mortals to understand, never mind accomplish? The answer you give in an academic essay (though not, perhaps, in a church) will depend – on what you're writing about, what you believe, and what you think your reader believes (or might be *willing* to believe).

I've been emphasizing all along here that writing history depends – depends much more than, say, writing poetry – on reading those documents we know as sources. But I want to end this particular discussion, and make the transition to talking about conclusions, by noting that writing history is also very much about thinking – of considering not only those documents, but your relationship to them, your relationship to the person you're addressing, and that person's relationship to the documents (which may or may not be the same as your own). Some of this, like writing poetry, may well be instinctive. But a sense of consciousness, and active choices, are crucial.

Is this complicated? You bet it is. And yet the mere art of being aware – which this limited little book is trying to get you do to – is an important first step.

Now let's begin talking about last steps.

# Chapter 13
# Surprising Conclusions

- Motivated conclusions
- Taking the long view

Many military historians – and many non-military historians – consider British historian John Keegan's *The Face of Battle* to be a masterpiece of twentieth-century historiography. Clearing his way through the thicket of conventions of his field as he inherited it, Keegan sought to explore the overlooked question of how combat was experienced at the ground level by ordinary soldiers by focusing on three European battles: Agincourt in 1415; Waterloo in 1815; and the Somme in 1916. His answer is that while all these (and many other) battles, were defined by similar experiences of dealing with fear, injury and death, the nature of the weapons – hand-held swords or lances at Agincourt; single-shot muskets or rifles at Waterloo; and machine guns or chemical weapons at the Somme – demarcate three crucially different warfare experiences.

In the final chapter of *The Face of Battle*, Keegan discusses developments in modern warfare since World War II. As he has noted all along, military historians tend to think about their subject in terms of decisive outcomes on the battlefield, or major political changes that follow major engagements. But, he says, the real significance of wars lies in the way they affect the psyches of individuals in society. The experience of two world wars and their aftermath have led the young people of Keegan's time – his book was published in 1976, which means it was taking shape amid the social movements of the 1960s – to reject traditional warfare altogether. He ends by saying

> It remains for armies to admit that the battles of the future will be fought in never-never land. While the great armoured hosts face each other across the boundary between east and west, no soldier on either side will concede that he does not believe in the function for which he plans and trains. As long as states put weapons in their hands, they will show each other the iron face of war. But the suspicion grows that battle has already abolished itself.[1]

After a discussion of 343 pages, *The Face of Battle* concludes with a suggestion that battle itself is obsolete. Most of the young people who constitute armies are no longer willing to fight; the few who are willing find themselves in a situation – Keegan's allusion to "east and west" refers to the militarized Cold War boundary in Germany – where, thanks to the nuclear deterrent of Mutually Assured Destruction (MAD), their training and equipment are largely beside the point. Not only are the battles Keegan chronicles history, but, he suggests, military history *itself* is history.

One would not expect a book by a military historian – a man who at the time of the book's publication and for decades afterward taught at a military institute, no less – to suggest that the very experiences that have been chronicled, and underlying continuities that have been traced, are not only obsolete, but irrelevant. A kind of melancholy air suffuses the end of *The Age of Battle*. It's as if Keegan is saying he's going to miss traditional warfare. He's far too sophisticated a historian, with far too vivid an imagination in depicting the horrors of combat, for this to come off as a glib attitude. (Actually, he would go on to write *A History of Warfare*, a strikingly original account of the subject that argues for war as an essential expression of the human experience.[2]) So while you may not agree with him, you still find yourself reflecting on what he has to say.

[1]   John Keegan, *The Face of Battle* (1976; New York: Penguin, 1978), 343.
[2]   John Keegan, *A History of Warfare* (New York: Knopf, 1993).

One reads the closing paragraphs of *The Face of Battle*, then, feeling that the author has given the reader a kind of bonus. You were told what to expect (by what you read on the cover, by the table of contents, by the long introductory chapter, and the like) and then you got something you didn't expect, too. That's what the best history does.

And that includes the best history essays. You're at a point in your academic career now where simply writing a report isn't quite enough. The prototypical report has a structure in which the introduction says, "This is what I'm going to tell you"; the body says, "Here I am telling you what I said I would"; and the conclusion says, "And now I'm repeating my summary point and telling you that everything I said is true." In a truly analytic essay, the intro doesn't tell: it asks. And the body doesn't tell either: it shows. The conclusion does to some degree sum up, but the goal now is to *extend* – to suggest the broader implications of the argument you've been making.

## Motivated Conclusions

Another way of saying this is that the conclusion is really the home of the motive of an essay. Questions are in the realm of the introduction. Theses get elaborated in the body. To some extent, both are vessels of the motive, which should be hinted at in the intro (typically in the final sentence or two) and sustained in the body (often in topic sentences). But what is suggested and/or implied in these earlier sections of an essay should be expressed more explicitly, with more elaboration, in the conclusion.

Let me give you an example. I recently had a student who wrote a research essay on the Spanish–American War. He took a very skeptical view of the war, whose origins he attributed to economic greed and a cavalier attitude toward human life on the part of U.S. policymakers. Toward the end of his introduction, this student wrote, "In the bigger picture of American involvement in foreign affairs, it is never appropriate for the United States to involve themselves for any reason except to protect themselves or unless a situation becomes so dire that it is absolutely necessary for them to intervene (World War II), which was not the case in the Spanish–American War." Here the antiwar motive is hinted at, an intriguing suggestion to pique a reader's curiosity even as the essay moves toward a more concrete and focused discussion of documentary evidence.

The body of the essay focuses, as it should, on origins, progress, and resolution of the Spanish–American War. The penultimate paragraph quotes Theodore Roosevelt, one of the war's strongest proponents, admitting in retrospect that his zeal got the better of his judgment ("Yes, I was right to go, although I suppose, at the bottom I was merely following my instinct instead of my reason," he quotes Roosevelt as saying.) It's a nice piece of evidence, and could conceivably have been a place to end the essay. But this writer is fishing for bigger game.

"What can we take away from the Spanish American War?" he begins his final paragraph. This strategy of posing a question here is a good one; it both anticipates what a reader is likely to be wondering as well as signaling that the end of the essay, with a strong finish, is at hand. His answer is that "the freedom of others does not justify the deaths of American soldiers," both because such a justification is likely to be distorted and because political leaders do not have the right to spill domestic blood for abstract foreign purposes.

Such a motive, articulated while a foreign war with Iraq was raging, had obvious and pointed relevance. But the writer was going further to articulate what he believed should be a general rule of U.S. foreign policy going forward as well – what some would call "isolationism." Whether or not his teacher agreed with this student's analysis (and here I must say I have reservations about drawing too straight a line between the Spanish–American War and the Iraq War), he is clearly drawing larger implications from his work in a way that adds interest, even drama, to his essay.[3]

Some historians remind us that we must respect the pastness of the past, and not read contemporary concerns too heavily into history, because we run the risk of distorting both the present and

---

[3]  Avery Wolff, "The Injustice of the Spanish-American War," written for Jim Cullen's U.S. History Survey, the Fieldston School, June 2007. Essay in the collection of the author.

the past when we do so. That's a point well taken. But it's also a risk I'm willing to run in the quest to develop informed, engaged, and active citizens – and vigorous writers.

## Taking the Long View

Of course not all conclusions must involve the writer dispensing advice to political leaders, or instructing readers to change their behavior (thank goodness). Sometimes a conclusion can simply pull back and put the material being analyzed in a broader perspective – to trace a border of forest after immersion in the trees. I once read a very good student essay about an overlooked gem of a movie, *Ride with the Devil* (1999), which focuses on guerilla warfare in Kansas and Missouri during the Civil War. This writer's thesis, unveiled in his introduction, is that the movie depicts "an ideological struggle between two parties with opposing definitions of freedom." At the end of the introduction, he notes, "In presenting these opposing perspectives, Ang Lee, a Taiwanese director, brings a unique interpretation of the Civil War." The body of the essay zeroes in on ideological conflict, and the ways it gets expressed itself even in realms that are presumably non-political (like marriage customs).

In the conclusion of the piece, however, the writer returns to the director. After recapitulating the thesis by saying "Confederate defeat ensured the Northern concept of liberty and changed America's ideology," he notes that for the screenplay of the film, Lee made small changes in the novel on which the movie was based and describes their impact. He concludes,

> In these somewhat marginal, but powerful, moments, Lee advances his position that the Civil War was one of ideology. As a Taiwanese director, his view is less tainted by American culture. Sensitive to the effects of globalization and at times sympathetic to the South, he finds the Civil War to be the beginning of America's modern history.[4]

---

[4] Rocky Russo, "*Ride with the Devil:* A Reconsideration of the Civil War through the Guerilla Conflict," written for Jim Cullen's "Civil War" class, the Fieldston School, May 26, 2005. Essay in the author's collection.

The movie doesn't only offer us a fresh interpretation of the Civil War, this essayist is saying. It also helps us understand the Civil War and American history itself from a broader (global) perspective, suggestive of tribal conflicts we often see in developing nations. That's a revealing and graceful cadence on which to end a piece of writing, and something you should strive for.

How? It goes back to that forest and trees metaphor. After a sustained period sifting through evidence, and sequencing it for the sake of your reader, you really need to step back as you come to the end of the body of an essay. Ask yourself: Now that I think I know what I'm saying, what does it all mean? Why does it matter?

One good strategy is to turn that question into a declarative sentence: It matters because.... The word *because* is important. Indeed, some teachers define a motive as an assertion that has the word "because" in it.[5] Does your thesis matter because it allows us to see the past differently (how)? Does it matter because it changes our perception of a current situation (how)? Does it matter because it's changed *you* (how?) in a way your reader may find useful or revealing? The answers to these kinds of questions lead to substantial and satisfying conclusions.

Of course, by this point in the process you may well be limping toward the finish line. When I'm making a first pass through an essay, I'm often desperate just to say I have a draft, and will walk away from a conclusion that I know is pretty weak. It's important to get something down, but it's also important not to dwell on it at this point, either. Often you need a little time – ideally a night – to let it percolate at the back of your mind while you do your laundry, make dinner, or even go out with friends. In any event, you need to start to think about the totality of your essay, to consider it whole. You may always be aware of the imperfections, but that doesn't mean your reader should be, or must be.

We're now entering the final phase of the writing process: revision. Done right, it's really the best part. Let's go there.

---

[5] I'm indebted to one of my colleagues, Kate Reynolds, a dean and member of the English Department at the Fieldston School, for this insight.

# Chapter 14

# Writing is Rewriting: The Art of Revision

- Conversation counts
- The writer as hotel manager
  - Burnish your prose
  - Do some stitching
  - Read your essay aloud
  - Tighten the framing
  - Settle on a title
  - Seek out a friendly critic

People like me writing books like this are fond of comparing an essay to a conversation. That makes a lot of sense, except, of course, that a conversation takes place in real time and an essay does not – an essay takes longer to write than it does to read, and it's read later (sometimes a lot later) than it's written. Actually, that's one of the great things about writing – it's conversation that allows its participants the illusion of transcending time, a phenomenon that's particularly satisfying in the realm of history, which is, in so many ways, time-bound. Actually, it's *ineluctably* time-bound; I speak of the *illusion* of transcending time, because essays are written in time, are read in time, and most of them get very dated, if not irrelevant, very quickly. But there's always the hope of saying something with a little more permanence than spoken words that evaporate into the air. You can't blame a historian (an American historian, anyway) for dreaming.

## Conversation Counts

But if writing an essay is a form of conversation, it's important to make clear that it isn't a two-person conversation or – acknowledging the intimacy of the writer–reader relationship – isn't *only* a two-person conversation. Actually, there are three classes of people involved in the creation of any essay: your sources, yourself, and your reader. Each of these classes is vitally important throughout the process, but each has a phase in that process where their role is primary. This is a good moment to reiterate, and clarify, this important point.

The first set of people you need to care about are those whose voices emerge from your sources. Some of those people are your subjects, whose ideas and feelings are captured in primary source documents. Others within this set are historians and other commentators who have worthwhile things to say in secondary sources. In the earliest stage of producing a piece of history, your job is to pay careful attention to what they think *on their terms*. You want to know and understand what they're saying, and you want to know from the point of view of the world as they knew it. You can't expect them to know or care about things that happened that they did not witness or live to see, and you can't assume that the things which are important to you are important to them, or important in the same way. Human beings typically care for their young, for example, but a loving parent in Moghul India did not necessarily conceive her role the same way one in ancient Egypt did – or refer to motherhood as a "role."

Once you move outside of research mode and begin to draft your essay, you continue to consider your sources, but your emphasis shifts away from what *they're* saying to what *you* want to say – what I call **writerly mode**. You should respect your sources, and you should work hard not to falsify or distort them. But at this point, you're the star and the sources are your supporting players. You're in the process of saying something that's never been said before in quite the way you're saying it.

After you've got a draft of an essay and reach the point we're focusing on here, on the revision process, the emphasis shifts again. Now you should be thinking primarily not of your sources or yourself, but of your reader. (There may be more than one, but in my experience it's always a particular imagined person with widely shared attributes, among them at least a casual interest in the topic you're discussing.) This is what I call ***readerly mode***. Your primary task now is to think about your sources and your ideas and the best way to present them so that *she* will understand – *and that she will care.*

Though in fact you're often juggling all three of these balls while not being conscious of it, each of these phases in the writing process involves a different set of skills, and true mastery of each of them requires conscious effort and reflection. And that takes time. I really can't repeat this point enough: Writing is rewriting. If you don't give yourself a sufficient opportunity for each phase of the process, with breaks in between, your essay simply won't be good. The weakest link is likely to be the one you can't afford to lose: the connection to the reader. I've read plenty of essays that have been written the day before or night before they're due, and they are almost always weak (and when they're not, they're often case studies in lost opportunity and unrealized potential). More than that: they're irritating as hell. I really resent reading work that seems to takes more work to read than it took to write, particularly when I'm slogging through dozens at a time. And I, like most teachers, am apt to penalize you for that.

## The Writer as Hotel Manager

I sometimes tell my students than in submitting an essay that they should liken themselves to a manager in a luxury hotel. The essay is the building; the reader is the guest who pays you with precious, undivided attention. The writer's job is to make life as pleasant as possible for that reader. The introduction, like a lobby, should gleam with clean prose. The body should have clear signs to direct the reader via elegant topic sentences, and the evidence should satisfy like a rich meal. The reader should finish the conclusion feeling like the visit was worthwhile (and, perhaps, meriting a return trip – or a stay at another hotel managed by the same company).

There are a number of tactics you should use as you revise your essay to achieve this sense of good management. Here are a few, in no particular order:

**Burnish your prose.** Nobody I know generates elegant writing from scratch – it always takes some polishing. This is particularly true in writing research essays, because the drafting process should place more primacy on getting good ideas down on paper than having those ideas smoothly expressed. (Indeed, trying too hard to get it right from the start is a prescription for writer's block.) But once you feel like you know what you want to say, then it's time to start thinking about achieving clarity and concision.

The first thing you want to do on this front is weed out words and phrases that bear the marks of thinking out loud. For example, there's rarely cause to use the phrase "I think" in a sentence, as in "I think Alexander the Great was one of the most versatile generals in the ancient world." We know what you think – you're saying so. Similarly, be on the lookout for locutions like "the fact of the matter is," or "irregardless of the circumstances," which are what I call "empty calories": lots of verbiage but little intellectual nutrition.

You should also be seeking opportunities to give your prose more punch by using active verbs instead of passive language. Don't say "a large force under the supervision of King Darius headed for an engagement with Greek forces"; say "King Darius spearheaded a large-scale attack against the Greeks." Instead of, "There was a growing need on the part of the army to requisition supplies to feed the troops," go with "Hunger sapped the army's strength." There are times when you may need to use the passive voice, particularly when you don't really know who or what is responsible for an observable phenomenon ("there were indications in the local press of growing sentiment in favor of a general strike"), but be conscious of actually making such a choice rather than lapsing into it. All of these considerations fall into the category of diction (see chapter 9).

**Do some stitching.** As mentioned in chapter 10, stitching refers to words and phrases that help link the various parts of an essay together. Double signposts (see chapter 10) are one form of stitching commonly employed in topic sentences. There are others, too, like repeating key terms throughout an essay or using parallel structures (like, for example "The most positive development to come about at the Congress of Vienna was ...." followed by "The most negative development to come about at the Congress of Vienna was ...."). Stitching may emerge naturally out of the drafting process, but it's in revision where you're most likely to be aware of the need, or even the opportunity, to bind your work into a more cohesive whole.

**Read your essay aloud.** There are few better strategies for getting a sense of how your work is going to be received than in hearing it aloud, even if the reader is yourself. Awkward or confusing phrases will be obvious, because you'll stumble over them. So will monotonous prose larded with lots of abstract words and jargon.

The main thing you want to get from reading aloud is a sense of *rhythm*. Writing sounds best when a writer provides variety in the length of sentences. Paragraphs composed of nothing but short sentences sound choppy; paragraphs with nothing but long ones get tiring and confusing. Don't be afraid of short, declarative sentences. But make sure that you break up others with clauses, like this, that offer a sense of flow to your reader.

**Tighten the framing.** I use the word "frame" to refer to the introduction and conclusion as a unit, "framing" to refer more generally to the alignment of the introduction, topic sentences, and conclusion of an essay as a whole. They're spaced apart from one end to the other, but in fact should have a tight, symbiotic relationship. Yet you can't fully understand that relationship until you've actually completed a draft. Now it's time to ask: Have you fully addressed the question you raise in the intro by the time you reach the conclusion? Is your thesis really what you said it was, or has it evolved or shifted since you first articulated it? If your thesis *has* changed, do the topic sentences reflect your current thinking?

This effort at realignment is particularly important in the realm of motive. Typically a motive only fully comes into focus late in the process, receiving its fullest articulation in the conclusion.

So it's a good idea to make sure that you add (or revise) indications of where you're headed in the introduction to reflect what you in fact go on to say in the conclusion.

You may also want to strengthen your motive in the body of the essay by choosing verbs and adjectives that "ionize" your prose with valences that reflect your larger attitude toward your subject. Instead of saying relatively neutrally that someone "did not take steps" prior to an unexpected event, you may now want to say more decisively that he "failed to anticipate" it. A historian's assessment that you agree with may become "impressively sober"; one you don't may now become what we can now see as a "premature" judgment. You don't want to lard up your prose with lots of unnecessary adjectives, but adding a choice word or two here and there can often go a long way in clarifying your stance toward a person or situation you're describing.

**Settle on a title.** Not all essay assignments require you to come up with an original title for your essay. But I think you should anyway. A good title will encapsulate your thesis, hint at your motive, and lure in a reader. The effort to generate one is an excellent tool for ascertaining what you have said in your essay, what you mean to say, and whether the two align.

Sometimes you think you know the answer to these questions, but when you step back you realize that they're not what you think. The first title for this book was going to be *Starting to Click: How to Write History – and Why You Would Want to*. I liked the play on the word "click," which referred to both the mouse on a computer as well process that's really beginning to gather momentum – to click. But on further reflection, I realized that "Starting to Click" doesn't refer at all to history, which is kind of a problem, since the marketing people would need a discipline-specific handle in order to convince historians that it made sense for them to order the book for students in a history course. (I was also never quite comfortable with a title that had a dangling preposition; though I wanted to come across as pragmatic and accessible, "why you would want to" is just a tad too informal). So then I came up with *Essaying the Past: How to Write History*. A little less lively, perhaps, but accurate and concise. But as I began to draft the chapters, I found myself realizing more and more that developing writing skills also involved developing reading skills. So I changed the subtitle to *How to Read and Write History*. And then, as I was drafting the later chapters I realized that *thinking*, an ongoing process and bridge between reading and writing, was central to the process of writing history, and reflected my general pedagogical vision as a whole, something which I resolved to explain in an introduction I hadn't yet written (the piece I'd drafted which I thought was going to be the introduction turned into chapter 1). So that's how you ended up reading this book with the title it has. Once *I* felt confident I knew what my title actually was, I used it as a kind of reference point for testing the cohesion and tautness of the manuscript as it went through multiple revisions.

**Seek out a friendly critic.** There's a fact I purposely omitted from my account of how I came up with the title of this book. And that is that I didn't do it alone. I had an editor, named Peter Coveney, who read and commented on my work, giving me support as well as advice. I was lucky. Hopefully you'll have such a resource too. Ideally, it will be your teacher, who will have both sufficient kindness and time to give you the attention you want and need.

Unfortunately, you can't always count on that. So it's worth trying to find someone else who might serve the role, at least until you hand in your essay. I said, and it's true, that reading an essay aloud to yourself can approximate what it might sound like to somebody else. But the best way to get a sense of how it sounds to somebody else is to actually find somebody else before you declare yourself finished.

There are three basic questions you should seek answers to from this reader without saying so beforehand:

1. What am I saying in this essay? What's my argument?
2. How do I make my argument? What's my approach to the sources I use?
3. Do you agree with what I say? (You should be as interested in the basis for a reader's agreement with you as a disagreement.)

Your first concern in learning your reader's answer to these questions is that they *can* be answered, that you're coherent enough to be understood. Confusion is a bigger problem than disagreement, and you should resist any impulse you may have to argue with your reader rather than to clarify your intentions – and to seek help in gauging what you need to say in order to be understood.

Of course, there's a correlation between the likelihood that you'll find yourself a good reader and your willingness to be one yourself. Reading your peers' essays isn't always fun, but it can be a valuable experience for you no less than for the writer of an essay you read. Seeing the choices other people make is a great way of clarifying your own. And as I've been saying all along, the essence of writing is choices.

And conversation. Ours is almost complete.

# Chapter 15

# Putting It All Together:
# The Research Essay
# (A Case Study)

My admonition that writing is rewriting applies no less to the writers of books than writers of essays, and it should come as no surprise to you that this book has been through multiple drafts and received multiple critiques from students, teachers, and editors. One of the pieces of feedback I got from a variety of sources was a wish that I would step back from the various components of writing an essay like introductions, evidence, and the like and talk about an essay as a whole, particularly in terms of how these various pieces fit together. At one point it had been my intention to generate a student essay myself, with running commentary on how I might choose to research, outline, and draft it. But it didn't take me long to realize that a hypothetical example of this type would not be as good as the real thing. So I'm going to give you one.

   The example I've chosen comes from my former student Katie Martell, who graduated from the Ethical Culture Fieldston School in 2008 and enrolled at Vanderbilt University later that year. I thought Katie's work would furnish a good illustration not simply because she's a good writer (as defined by the standards I've been outlining in the previous pages), but because I witnessed her *become* one over a period of months. Like you, Katie was an intelligent person with basic skills and a desire to improve. Writing assignments were a source of some anxiety, and she found it difficult to assert herself with confidence (sometimes she still does, I would guess). But she worked hard, focused on some of the techniques discussed here, and by the time she graduated could routinely express herself with clarity.

Before introducing her work and my running commentary on it, allow me to say a few words about the context for the following essay. It was the culmination of a course I taught in the fall of 2007 entitled "A Life in Time: Biography as History." The class consisted of a series of case studies of a wide range of figures that ranged from Genghis Khan to Elvis Presley. For each person we studied, we looked at multiple sources that were arranged around a particular question (that could be answered multiple ways, like "What did Julius Caesar do?" or "What did freedom mean to [Caribbean slave] Mary Prince?" In the final segment of the course, students were told to choose a figure, formulate a question, and answer it in a research essay.

Here's how Katie began her project:

> I chose Malcolm X because I wanted to write about someone who was clearly controversial and also someone who I wasn't extremely knowledgeable about. I have learned a great deal about Martin Luther King Jr., but I realized that I knew almost nothing about Malcolm X besides that fact that he believed in complete segregation between blacks and whites. I started by forming a question that I knew could be argued well from both sides. Before I chose which side I was going to argue I wanted to learn more basic information about Malcolm X and then from that figure out how I wanted to shape my argument. I watched the movie Malcolm X, read excerpts from his autobiography and as embarrassing as this is I also used Wikipedia, but just a little.

Katie generated a bibliography for her essay. Normally, of course, such a document goes at the end of an essay (see appendix A). But since we're explaining how it was constructed, and because her bibliography is annotated – she describes why these sources were useful to her – it makes sense to begin rather than end with it.

## Katie's Bibliography

Archer, Jules. *They Had a Dream: The Civil Rights Struggle from Frederick Douglass to Marcus Garvey to Martin Luther King, Jr. and Malcolm X.* Penguin Young Readers Group, 1996.

This book contains four biographies. Historian Jules Archer presents the stories of courage and determination and the history of the civil rights struggle in the United States. From this book I learned about the lives of Frederick Douglass, Marcus Garvey, Martin Luther King Jr., and Malcolm X. The book helped me see the involvement and effect that the three men had on the Civil Rights movement, in comparison to Malcolm X. I also think it is important to read about Malcolm X from an outside perspective and not just an autobiography.

King, Jr. Martin Luther. *Papers of Martin Luther King, Jr.,* Stanford University. http://www.stanford.edu/group/King/publications/papers/unpub/650226-001_To_Betty_Shabazz.htm

This website was where I found a letter from King to Malcolm X's wife that I used in the essay.

Smith, Ray. "Malcolm X, 40 years after the death of a revolutionary." Marxist. 21 Feb 2005. http://www.marxist.com/History/malcolmx_revolutionary.htm

This website is where I found Malcolm X's comments on the assassination of John F. Kennedy Jr.

X, Malcolm. "Harvard University Address." *American Rhetoric.* http://www.americanrhetoric.com/MovieSpeeches/moviespeechmalcolmxharvard.html

I used this website in order to find excerpts from Malcolm X's speech at Harvard University.

———. "The House Negro vs The Field Negro." *Zimbio.* http://www.zimbio.com/Black+History+Month/articles/265/Malcolm+X+House+Negro+vs+Field+Negro

This is the website where I found Malcolm X's speech in which he speaks about "The House Negro vs. The Field Negro."

———. *Malcolm X Speaks.* New York: Grove Press, 1994

This book is comprised of the major speeches made by Malcolm X during the last eight months of his life. In this short period of time, his vision for abolishing racial inequality in the United States underwent a huge transformation. Beginning with his break from the Black Muslims, he moved increasingly away from the beliefs of Black Nationalism, separatism, and violent revolution as the only means to achieve freedom. He accepted a broader view of human rights, and at least the possibility of alliances with other groups. This book was a great source for seeing the shift in Malcolm X's effect on the Civil Rights movement and on race relations.

———— with Alex Haley. *The Autobiography of Malcolm X.* 1965; New York: Ballantine Books, 1992.

This book tells the story of the life of Malcolm X and the growth of the Black Muslim movement, from the words of Malcolm X, to veteran writer and journalist Alex Haley. The book gave me a great understanding of his background and also the teachings of Elijah Muhammad, which Malcolm X devoted himself to. It helped me decipher his message and the way in which it was spread from Malcolm X himself. From it I better understood what the reactions were to him from both sides of the Civil Rights spectrum and the controversy that followed him.

Malcolm X." *Wikipedia.* 11 January 2008. http://en.wikipedia.org/wiki/Malcolm_X#Nation_of_Islam

I used this website for some of my basic background information on Malcolm X and this is where I found the famous quote where Malcolm X speaks about the March on Washington as "the farce on Washington."

Katie collected and sifted through these sources over a matter of weeks. She learned things she didn't know; she found information that confirmed some of her ideas; she found other information that challenged her ideas. But she was able to move toward a preliminary assessment:

As I learned about Malcolm X and his life I was very torn because I quickly recognized what a great man he was, especially the fact that he could acknowledge his mistakes and learn from them. But I also saw the negative aspects of his actions. I realized that the extremity of his negative qualities outweighed his positive ones and this in turn crippled his ability to do great things for the Civil Rights movement.

Now it was time to draft. Here's what she was thinking as she began to write:

I started with an introduction. In the introduction I wanted to make clear how I defined the key terms I would be using. I was arguing that Malcolm X had an overall negative effect on race relations and if I was going to do that, the reader had to know what I believed to be a positive effect. I introduced both sides of the argument and then stated my thesis.

Here's how her essay opens:

Did Malcolm X have a positive or negative effect on race relations? Before delving into the question at hand, it is important to understand what exactly constitutes a positive effect on race relations. Is it better to foster peaceful relations between blacks and whites, despite the obvious inequities of American society, or is it better to incite outrage and division so that these inequities are brought to light and ended? One of the reasons why Americans found Malcolm X to be such a potentially dangerous figure is because he did not want to wait patiently for America to dismantle a racist cultural framework that had existed since the nation's founding. Malcolm X was not a fan of slow reform; he wanted to tear down the walls and break the shackles that had imprisoned his people politically and intellectually for over three centuries. Unfortunately, Malcolm X's brand of political candor was only designed to incite and not to heal ....

Having an introduction to work with was important in its own right, but it was also valuable to Katie because it helped her figure out where to go from there.

From this introduction I formed my outline. I knew that Malcolm's life was broken up into clear stages and I wanted to walk through these stages in my paragraphs, while presenting evidence and insight to support my argument. While outlining the paragraphs I found myself using the background information I had found at the start of my research and then analyzing it in an unstructured form, just to get it on the page. I broke my paragraphs up into what I thought would explain the key points of his life that best supported my thesis. They were:

- Childhood
- Descent into criminality
- First glimpse of Islam when in prison

- Career as activist
  - Fight with Martin Luther King, Jr.
  - Call for self-sufficiency
  - Comments on Kennedy assassination
- Ramifications of Malcolm's actions
- Ballot or the bullet speech
- Moderating his politics/trip to Mecca
- Consequences of moderation
- Conclusion

I'll have observations of my own to offer when I reproduce the essay in full. But first, a few more words on where Katie went from here:

> Once I had completed this outline, I went back to fill in facts, quotes, topic sentences, and connecting sentences. I wanted everything to flow so I made sure that all my paragraphs fed into each other and had a clear purpose. It was also important to have a supporting fact or quote in each paragraph and to make clear what that fact or quote was contributing to my argument.

OK. Now it's time to see what she did. At the end of each paragraph is a box in which I analyze the choices she's just made.

A word about the title: It was a suggestion to Katie that I made, which she accepted. Originally, her title was "Did Malcolm X Have a Positive or Negative Effect on Race Relations?" I thought that "Every Means Is Not Necessary," a play on Malcolm's famous assertion that African Americans should assert themselves "by any means necessary," encapsulates her thesis, while "The Tragedy of Malcolm X" points to her motive. Her question, I argued, would be a good way to get the essay off to a fast start. Could you argue that this was my idea and not hers? In some sense, yes. But it's an idea that grew directly of out what I read in her work, and receiving as well as accepting advice is central to the writing process. In every sense that really matters, this is Katie Martell's work. And other than copy-editing intervention like correcting typos, the ideas and execution are entirely hers.

Every Means Is Not Necessary: The Tragedy of Malcolm X
By Katie Martell

Did Malcolm X have a positive or negative effect on race relations? Before delving into the question at hand, it is important to understand what exactly constitutes a positive effect on race relations. Is it better to foster peaceful relations between blacks and whites, despite the obvious inequities of American society, or is it better to incite outrage and division so that these inequities are brought to light and ended? One of the reasons why Americans found Malcolm X to be such a potentially dangerous figure is because he did not want to wait patiently for America to dismantle a racist cultural framework that had existed since the nation's founding. Malcolm X was not a fan of slow reform; he wanted to tear down the walls and break the shackles that had imprisoned his people politically and intellectually for over three centuries. Unfortunately, Malcolm X's brand of political candor was only designed to incite and not to heal. The effects of slavery and institutionalized racism in the United States had seeped into virtually every aspect of American society and could not be purged purely through righteous anger. Malcolm X's approach to civil rights was idealistic to the point that it lacked any sense of political subtlety or compromise. It is ironic that it took a political betrayal by his fellow black nationalists in the Nation of Islam for Malcolm X to moderate his politics. It was only at this point that Malcolm X was able to realize that the only way to change the system was to work with it and pose an implicit rather than an explicit threat to the existing power structure of the country. The tragedy of Malcolm X is that he had created such an air of controversy around him that by the time he had crafted his true message, it was too late.

There are a number of things going right in this introduction. The first, as noted regarding the title, is that the question the essay is trying to answer is foregrounded. To be sure, the question that animates any essay doesn't always have to come first thing; indeed, there are times where you might need to establish a fact or lay out a premise before you can pose a question. But the one here is direct, compelling, and even dramatic, since you can't tell at the outset exactly which way Katie will go.

The second good choice Katie makes is in moving quickly to define her terms. She makes clear that there are two ways to define

135

better race relations, and a dilemma in each one (accepting inequity as the price of peace or generating discord as the price of change) and that both have at least some merit. This again generates interest: Which fork in the road will she choose?

The third good thing is that she answers this question quickly and cleanly: She notes that Malcolm took the latter road, but that she regards it as "idealistic to the point that it lacked any sense of political subtlety or compromise." This critical stance toward Malcolm is the essence of her thesis – though, as we'll see, she maintains a sense of fairness and balance that typifies the strength of her liberal approach.

Finally, Katie also tips her hand toward a motive. She doesn't actually say why the question continued to matter directly, but her use of the word "tragedy" in the context of Malcolm's life, denoting an unhappy outcome that might have been otherwise, implies that there's a lesson or warning we can take from his experience.

In sum, we have the complete rhetorical package here, and can go forward confident that we have a driver who both knows the terrain and will move us forward without a lot of wasted motion.

---

Malcolm X was not only an important activist but an example of the sheer scope of the African American experience in this country. He was both victim and victimizer; agitator and activist; destructive and provocative. To truly understand Malcolm X's political outlook later in life, it is necessary to take several key snapshots of his early years and relate them to the black struggle in America. Malcolm's first experience with racism came when he was still in the womb and the Ku Klux Klan broke the windows of his house because his father, Earl Little, a Baptist minister, was involved with the Universal Negro Improvement Association. Malcolm's life began in an environment of racial intolerance and violence. Eventually his father's political beliefs provoked further reprisals from other white supremacist groups that resulted in the burning of his family home in Lansing, Michigan. Malcolm's earliest memories include observing as "the white police and fireman came and stood around watching as the house burned down to the ground."[1] The juxtaposition of the burning house with the police and firemen, representatives of the civil government, is a stirring symbol of the way in which society treated blacks like second-class

---

[1]   Malcolm X with Alex Haley, *The Autobiography of Malcolm X* (1965; New York: Ballantine 1992), 3.

citizens. Of course, the burning of his house pales when compared to the ultimate tragedy of his childhood, the murder of his father, which was ruled a suicide by the local authorities. This made it clear to Malcolm that any black man who attempted to reform the system would be met with violent hostility and death. Given this childhood experience, it is not surprising that Malcolm developed a disdain for white authority and chose to enter a life of crime.

---

In this second paragraph, Katie makes the transition from the introduction to the body of the essay. The first two sentences establish Malcolm X's significance in the broader context of African American history. But it's really the third sentence, "To truly understand Malcolm X's political outlook later in life, it is necessary to take several key snapshots of his early years and relate them to the black struggle in America," that establishes her signal strategy in the essay. And that strategy, as she indicated in her remarks above, is to construct an outline of Malcolm's life that highlights those moments that illustrate her thesis, i.e. his understandable, but misguided, radicalism. Thus it is that the remainder of the paragraph discusses a childhood in which he was led to conclude that "any black man who attempted to reform the system would be met with violent hostility and death." We now anticipate, correctly, that a series of other snapshots will follow.

---

Another important snapshot in Malcolm's life is his experience as a street hustler in Harlem. As he would later confess in many of his fiery speeches, a life of crime was the only option that he perceived was available to him. He believed that the institutionalized racism in the United States made it impossible for a black man to attain any measure of power, influence, or genuine standing, unless it was outside the limits of normal behavior. Speaking to a collection of Harvard Law School students, Malcolm stated, "In fact, my old burglary hangout is just outside this campus. I lived like an animal. I stole. I used drugs. I smoked reefers, cocaine. I committed adultery. Had it not been for the Honorable Elijah Muhammad, I'd of surely been in an insane asylum, or dead, or possibly even the murderer of one of you."[2] The last words of this quote resonate

---

[2] Malcolm X, "Harvard University Address." *American Rhetoric.* http://www.american rhetoric.com/MovieSpeeches/moviespeechmalcolmxharvard.html. Cited January 11, 2008.

because they are filled with allusions to the danger of creating an entire generation of disillusioned, disaffected, and angry black men. Malcolm is basically stating that deviance and criminality are merely the symptoms of the infectious disease that is the black American experience. The fact that Malcolm experienced the depths of being a criminal gave him an invaluable perspective that allowed him to relate to other black men who took a similar path or were considering it.

---

By now, Katie is hitting her stride in the body. One important indicator of this is the topic sentence of this paragraph, anchored at the top. Note also that she uses a classic double signpost in her phrase, "another important snapshot in Malcolm's life." This reminds the reader of the previous snapshot (the violent death of his father) and connects it to the next one (his career as a street hustler). These cues give the essay a strong sense of structure, something particularly welcome in a discussion that's both relatively long and analytic.

There's another pattern at work here, a tactic used in the second paragraph but even more obvious here and in every subsequent one of the body: Katie's three-step process for using primary source evidence in the form of quotes. First, she sets up any quotation by identifying the context (here it's "speaking to a collection of Harvard Law School students"). Then she actually quotes the source, which happens to be the celebrated *Autobiography of Malcolm X*. Then she actually quotes the source, which happens to be the celebrated *Autobiography of Malcolm X*. Then she follows up by making explicitly clear how the quote relates to her thesis: "The last words of this quote resonate because ...." The sturdiness of this construction, used repeatedly, helps her reader stay focused and demonstrates a kind of diligence that adds to her credibility.

---

The penultimate experience of Malcolm's transformation came during the period in which he was incarcerated at the Massachusetts state prison and later the Norfolk prison colony. While at Norfolk, Malcolm was introduced to the brand of Islam by his family, practiced by followers of Elijah Mohammed. It was at this point that Malcolm Little completely disappeared and was reincarnated as Malcolm X. Malcolm already had a clear distaste for the white power structure but the teachings of Elijah

Mohammed took this abstract sense of hatred and made it more focused. The Nation of Islam literally believed that all white people were devils. Malcolm X, the critical thinker that he was, did not immediately embrace this idea but came to accept it when he thought about all the white people he had known. He states in his autobiography, "The white people I had known marched before my mind's eye … the white judge and others who had split up the children … the teachers – the one who told me in the eighth grade to 'be a carpenter' because thinking of being a lawyer was foolish for a Negro … the cops … the white women who wanted Negro men … the judge who gave me ten years …".[3] The sheer scope of his experience with white America suggests a pattern of subjugation and betrayal that made Elijah Mohammed's teachings so appealing. In Malcolm's opinion, Christianity was yet another part of the white power structure. Islam allowed black men to live with a set of principles that fostered equality and proper behavior. Malcolm X stated that he was more free in prison than he had ever been, mostly because he was allowed the opportunity to educate himself. Upon his release from prison, Malcolm had become one of the nation's most eloquent speakers and deliverers of its message of Black Nationalism and separation.

---

This paragraph uses some of the strategies already discussed. Note, though, that the signpost in the topic sentence looks forward more than back – "penultimate" means next-to-last, reassuring the reader that the string of biographical snapshots is not going to continue indefinitely. Note too that while Katie sets up and follows through on her quotation, here she makes the active choice of streamlining her use of the Autobiography by inserting ellipses, tracking a list of all the people Malcolm remembered, but keeping that list concise and flowing by leapfrogging with key examples. One senses fidelity to the spirit of what her source is trying to say as well as its content.

---

Malcolm's arrival on the American political scene can reasonably be compared to the arrival of a hurricane or other force of nature. Malcolm crafted a very radical belief system which unequivocally portrayed the white population as the enemy. Although America was primarily a white society and therefore it wasn't much of a logical leap to say that whites were responsible for the oppression of blacks, this was not a rhetorical

---

[3] *The Autobiography of Malcolm X*, 163.

approach used by most civil rights leaders. In fact, leaders like Martin Luther King made a point of never casting the white population as villains. Most of these moderate activists tried to achieve a positive relationship with white political figures, so that they had allies in their struggle for equality. Malcolm made it clear that instead of working with the white population, he wanted to completely disconnect from them. He scoffed at the efforts of more moderate leaders like Martin Luther King and called the March on Washington, "the farce on Washington" and said that it was, "run by whites in front of a statue of a president who has been dead for a hundred years and who didn't like us when he was alive."[4] He believed that any strategy involving negotiating with the white government was counterproductive. As incendiary as this outlook was, it was based on historical fact. According to Malcolm X, another form of control the white population had used against the blacks since the days of slavery was to make certain black people more comfortable than others, creating the illusion that they were equal. Malcolm used the metaphor of the "House Negro" versus the "Field Negro" to illustrate this point. He stated:

> "There was two kind of slaves. There was the house Negro and the field Negro. The house Negro, they lived in the house, with master. They dressed pretty good. They ate good, cause they ate his food, what he left. They lived in the attic or the basement, but still they lived near their master, and they loved their master, more than their master loved himself. They would give their life to save their masters house quicker than their master would."[5]

The point that Malcolm was trying to make was that the subjugation of blacks by whites was not only explicit but implicit. It insidiously creates an inferiority complex within blacks and infantilizes them, making them want the approval and comfort of their "white superiors." Therefore, Malcolm distrusted any white people or white organizations, because as far as he was concerned their sole purpose was to control him and moderate his message until it meant nothing.

---

[4] "Malcolm X." *Wikipedia.* http://en.wikipedia.org/wiki/Malcolm_X#Nation_of_Islam. Cited January 11, 2008.
[5] Malcolm quoted in "Malcolm X: The House Negro vs. The Field Negro." *Zimbio.* http://www.zimbio.com/Black+History+Month/articles/265/Malcolm+X+House+Negro+vs+Field+Negro. Cited January 11, 2008.

This paragraph signals a transition within the body of the essay. Up until now, Katie has been focusing on the **causes** of Malcolm X's radicalism. Here, though, she's setting up a three-paragraph discussion on the **effects** of that radicalism as he moves into the heart of his career. She illustrates such effects by contrasting his career with that of Martin Luther King, Jr. and Malcolm's stance toward it (for example his dismissive description of the 1963 March on Washington as "the farce on Washington"). She continues her strategy of setting up and following through with quotes, but this time she makes the decision to use a block quote from an article Malcolm wrote, one which takes the form of a complete little anecdote about the house Negro and field Negro, noting the militance implicit in the tale.

What made Malcolm's message so problematic to both black and white politicians is the way in which he made the separation of the races a non-negotiable aspect of his political and social philosophy. This was a radically different approach to the civil rights struggle and made many people in the United States nervous. Malcolm was calling on all black people to sever their ties from the existing white power structure and strive to create a system of self sufficiency. Malcolm took issue with the fact that black Americans were rarely in control of the modes of production. In other words, there were too few black-owned businesses in the United States to give the black population any measure of economic power. Malcolm hoped to change that by instilling the spirit of Black Nationalism in his followers. Speaking of all black people, Malcolm stated, "We have a common enemy. We have this in common: We have a common oppressor, a common exploiter, and a common discriminator ... the white man."[6] The FBI took note of this phrasing and characterized Malcolm as someone who had the potential of inciting irreparable racial violence. The last thing that the existing power structure wanted was a black army within its borders that viewed the white majority as the enemy. Malcolm's message was also offensive to other civil rights leaders because it undercut their ability to gain support from moderate and liberal white Americans who believed in the cause of civil rights.

---

[6] Malcolm X, *Malcolm X Speaks* (New York: Grove Press, 1994), 5.

Up until now, Katie has been very careful to talk about Malcolm X largely on Malcolm X's terms. She's been trying to explain where he came from, what he believed, and why he believed what he did. But in opening this paragraph with a topic sentence that begins "What made Malcolm's message so problematic," she's signaling that the essay is moving decisively onto her terms, beginning a process of assessment necessary for any essay with a thesis that's explained as well as asserted. Because she's been so patient and attentive, we're eager for her to finally weigh in, and inclined to take her seriously because she's done her homework, both in doing her research and in setting us up to elaborate on her thesis. This feels like a turning point, which makes sense, since we're at about the halfway mark of the essay.

Although Malcolm's message was reaching wider audiences and he was winning many supporters, he was also alienating himself from many people who were sympathetic to the black cause. Malcolm seemed completely unconcerned about this situation and continued with his inflammatory rhetoric. Unfortunately, he had absolutely no capacity for self censorship and this proved detrimental when he commented on the assassination of President John F. Kennedy. It is important to note that JFK was a supporter of the Civil Rights movement, but, like many white politicians who had to weigh the opinions of the entire nation, he could not chart an aggressive course towards racial equality and instead promoted a more gradual process. This angered Malcolm X, who felt that JFK was yet another hypocrite who preached liberal values but was either unable or unwilling to put himself on the line for these convictions. When asked for a response to John F. Kennedy's murder, Malcolm said, "Chickens come home to roost. Being an old farm boy myself, chickens coming home to roost never did make me sad; they've always made me glad."[7] The implication of this statement was that JFK got what he deserved and something like that should never provoke sympathy. His comment was highly controversial because President Kennedy represented a new breed of young white liberals in the United States who truly wanted to change things. What Malcolm failed to realize was that there was no way for blacks in the United States to achieve equal rights

[7]  Ray Smith. "Malcolm X, 40 years after the death of a revolutionary." *Marxist*. 21 Feb. 2005. http://www.marxist.com/History/malcolmx_revolutionary.htm. Cited January 11, 2008.

if they antagonized the existing power structure. A certain level of protest was required, but beyond a certain point it became counterproductive. Malcolm had a valuable message, but it was often covered in a sheen of violence, which detracted from its significance. At this point even the Nation of Islam chose to distance itself from their premier representative.

---

Here we enter a passage of counterargument. Katie has noted a number of times in this essay (in the introduction, for example, and again in the fifth paragraph, where she notes that Malcolm's skepticism about the utility of negotiating with white government officials "was based on historical fact") that his radicalism was a plausible stance for he and his supporters to take. But here she notes it was ultimately mistaken, not on the basis of some abstract or neutral standard of morality, but because he was alienating some of the very people he was trying to help. She uses a well-known fact – that Malcolm's own Nation of Islam disavowed his remarks on the Kennedy assassination – as evidence to support her (counter)argument. That she does so at the end of the paragraph, in a short declarative sentence unembellished with clauses or extra punctuation, gives this evidence extra impact.

---

A perfect example of how Malcolm's valuable insights into American race relations was misinterpreted because of the violent imagery he used is in his "the Ballot or the Bullet" speech. In the speech Malcolm points out that although blacks technically had the right to vote, they suffered from de facto disenfranchisement. He insisted that there were so many institutional and cultural restrictions placed on black people, that their political voice had been reduced to a whisper. He actually turns this political issue into a human rights issue and said that if blacks were not given the right to vote, they would have to get that right violently, hence the word "bullet." He states, "That's why, in 1964, it's time now for you and me to become more politically mature and realize what the ballot is for; what we're supposed to get when we cast a ballot; and that if we don't cast a ballot, it's going to end up in a situation where we're going to have to cast a bullet. It's either a ballot or a bullet."[8] It is easy to understand why Malcolm chose the word "bullet"; at heart, he was a sensationalist who wanted his message to stir things up. Unfortunately, constantly stirring things up creates a sense of instability that did not result in any forward progress for the movement.

[8]  *Malcolm X Speaks*, 30.

This paragraph reinforces the counterargument of the previous paragraph with the additional example of his "the Ballot or the Bullet speech." In so doing, Katie demonstrates that the "Chickens come home to roost" remark cited earlier was not an isolated incident, but part of a larger pattern that confirms her thesis: Malcolm X went too far.

At some point Malcolm realized that his controversial political stance ran counter to his ultimate goals. This coincided with Malcolm's trip to Mecca and his separation from the Nation of Islam. He realized that Islam was a religion with a scope far greater than the African American population. In his journey to Mecca he met Muslims with blonde hair and blue eyes who shared his religious beliefs and who he came to respect and this completely changed his theories on racial segregation. In his travels Malcolm redefines the concept of "white" and this allows him to reassess his outlook. In his autobiography, Malcolm wrote:

> "That morning was when I first began to reappraise the 'white man.' It was when I first began to perceive that 'white man,' as commonly used, means complexion only secondarily; primarily it describes attitudes and actions. In America, 'white man' meant specific attitudes and actions towards the black man .... But in the Muslim world, I had seen that men with white complexions were more genuinely brotherly then anyone else had ever been."[9]

He decided that his movement could use the help of white people although he still insisted that they could never truly understand or join the black struggle. This attempt to moderate his politics was a sign that some of the righteous anger that had fueled his public life until that point had been replaced with a grudging pragmatism.

Here Katie's counterargument reaches a climax with her assertion in the topic sentence that Malcolm X himself recognized his tactical mistake. The topic sentence also advances her storyline by moving into her penultimate snapshot, this one of Malcolm in Mecca. This in effect marks the culmination of her work on her thesis, as we reach the end of the radical phase in Malcolm's life and his shift toward a more conciliatory style.

[9] *The Autobiography of Malcolm X*, 340.

Upon Malcolm's return to New York, he had completely changed the way he approached the Civil Rights movement. This is not to say that he adopted Martin Luther King's peaceful ways, but he certainly made himself available to King on many occasions as an advisor and advocate. Unfortunately Malcolm's moderate point of view may have seemed more like a threat to his assassins. If Malcolm were able to extend his unique brand of magnetic charisma to other moderate civil rights figures, those who wanted to slow the progression of civil rights would have had something to truly fear. Unfortunately for reasons that are still unknown, Malcolm became too much of a threat to certain extremists and he was assassinated on February 21, 1965. Malcolm's legacy was best described by Martin Luther King whose letter to Malcolm's widow read:

"I was certainly saddened by the shocking and tragic assassination of your husband. While we did not always see eye to eye on methods to solve the race problem, I always had a deep affection for Malcolm and felt that he had a great ability to put his finger on the existence and the root of the problem. He was an eloquent spokesman for his point of view and no one can honestly doubt that Malcolm had a great concern for the problems we face as a race."[10]

This quote manages to capture exactly what Malcolm was capable of doing, namely, pinpointing the glaring problems facing black people in the United States and publicizing these problems with almost immeasurable verve and power.

> Here Katie's sense of care and generosity remain in place as she heads toward the conclusion of this essay. All along she's been saying Malcolm took a mistaken path, but when he finally corrects it, she does not presume that he would agree with Martin Luther King (or Katie Martell) entirely. Her use of King to pay tribute to Malcolm suggests their shared values amid their divisions, a tribute that has credibility (there's that word again) in light of the clarity of previous criticism. Her lament of his death is sincere, as is her praise for what he could accomplish, whatever its limits.

[10] "Papers of Martin Luther King, Jr." Stanford University. http://www.stanford.edu/group/King/publications/papers/unpub/650226-001_To_Betty_Shabazz.htm. Cited January 11, 2008.

145

The question of whether Malcolm X had a positive or negative effect on race relations in America cannot be properly assessed without fully understanding what his effect was. Malcolm cannot be credited with solving any problems; his value to the Civil Rights movement was most directly related to his ability to focus his outrage at any and all individuals and groups complicit in the systematic oppression of black Americans. He had no qualms about transmitting information to the general public that could make them feel uncomfortable and this discomfort in turn filled people with a sense of impending catastrophe. Malcolm painted a picture of America which could possibly go up in flames if the rights and liberties of the black population were not recognized. Unfortunately, Malcolm's righteous anger peaked at a level that not only made those in power uncomfortable, but also negatively affected the opinions of Americans who were inclined to agree with this point of view. Although Black Nationalism made sense in theory, it was almost impossible to execute because of the deeply entrenched cultural, political, and social values of the nation. Once Malcolm realized that he couldn't take such an extreme approach to solving America's race problems, his moderation was of little or no consequence. He had already made so many potentially devastating comments that simply retracting them couldn't win back those he had alienated. In the end, a figure like Malcolm X was necessary to transmit the unfiltered truth, and in that sense he was a positive force. However, if he had moderated his politics sooner and worked within the system instead of against it, he may have been able to have a greater influence than Martin Luther King himself. Malcolm X leaves no notable heirs, yet his legacy of political courageousness and open mindedness serves as an excellent lesson to any activist facing insurmountable odds.

---

Katie's conclusion is marked by a strong sense of recapitulation. The very phrase "the question of whether Malcolm X had a positive or negative effect on race relations" harkens back to her introduction. She again emphasizes the possibilities as well as the limits of his militant approach to activism.

Yet the question remains: Why does any of this matter a half-century later? Is there any lesson in the life and death of Malcolm X, any sense of hope? In a way, no: Malcolm changed his ways, but it was too little, too late, and this truly is tragic. Implicit here is a suggestion, however, that later generations – like that of Katie and her peers – might be able to avoid his mistakes when they too combat the injustices of **their** time. Perhaps **they** can "moderate [their] politics

> sooner and work within the system instead of against it." But even as they might depart from the strategy of Malcolm X, Katie takes note of his "political courageousness and open-mindedness" that serve as a positive lesson alongside the cautionary tale.

Is "Any Means Is Not Necessary" a perfect essay? I don't think so, and I don't think Katie would assert as much either. My suspicion is that some of Katie's paragraphs could have been a bit tighter, and I would have liked to see her develop the largely implicit dimensions of her motive more explicitly, both in the introduction as well as the conclusion (which is to say that the frame of the essay could have been stronger). This is, nevertheless, an excellent piece of work – an A essay from an A student. Let's return to her for a few final comments.

The conclusion was very important and it needed to completely wrap up everything I had just thrown at the reader and give it meaning. I wanted to make clear that it was entirely possible that Malcolm X could have had an extremely positive effect on race relations but with the facts that I had presented and the information that I had fully analyzed he did not. I realized that at the end I did not have to fully understand the complex man that was Malcolm X but I understood what I was arguing and what I believed in as a result of my research and that, I think, is the most important thing to convey in an essay.

Katie's conclusions are, of course, arguable. That's precisely the point. She worked out where she finally comes down on the question she poses, and her deceptively simple essay, written with intelligence and insight, can help a reader do the same, whether or not that reader takes the same fork in the road that she does. In both her civility and her concern for the rights of others, this is an example of truly democratic discourse.

# Conclusion:
# The Love of History

> If this book should one day be published – if, begun as a simple antidote by which, amid sorrows and anxieties both personal and collective, I see a little peace of mind, it should turn into a real book, intended to be read – you will find, my friend, another name than yours inscribed on its dedication page .... Yet how can I resign myself to seeing you appear in no more than a few chance references? Long have we worked together for a wider and more human history. Today our common task is threatened. Not by our fault. We are vanquished, for a moment, by an unjust destiny. But the time will come, I feel sure, when our collaboration can again be public, and again be free.[1]

When Marc Bloch wrote these words to Lucien Febvre on May 10, 1941 – the two were instrumental figures in the formation of the Annales school of social history (see chapter 2) – the world was a very dark place. Bloch, a Jew, was a 53-year-old Professor of Economic History at the University of Paris when the Second World War began, at which point he joined the French army for the second time (he had also fought in the First World War). After the fall of Paris in 1940, he published a book, *Strange Defeat*, chronicling the rapid collapse of French forces to the Nazi juggernaut.

[1] Marc Bloch, *The Historian's Craft*, trans. By Peter Putnam (New York: Vintage, 1953), v. Much of the information for the subsequent biographical sketch comes from Joseph R. Strayer's introduction (vii–xii) and Lucien Febvre's note on the manuscript (xiii–xviii).

Although he could have fled at that point to the United States, Bloch chose to remain in the struggle, retreating to the nominally free Vichy France, taking university posts there, and joining the French resistance. When the Germans decided to overrun Vichy in 1942, Bloch was driven from academic life entirely. He was ultimately captured by the Germans, imprisoned, and tortured. On June 16, 1944, just as the D-Day invasion was beginning to wrest France from the Nazi grip, Bloch was taken from his jail cell and shot in an open field with 26 other resistance fighters.

It was in this fugitive phase of his life that Bloch began writing the unfinished book that Febvre would finish as *The Historian's Craft*. (Febvre explained that Bloch's quandary over the dedication stemmed from his desire to honor his wife, who also died in the French resistance). One can only imagine the tremendous adversity in which Bloch sought to distill his decades of experience as a historian, undoubtedly lacking many of the resources, bibliographic and otherwise, that a scholar would normally depend upon. It is a measure of his fierce devotion to his country – and his fierce devotion to the art of history, which he analyzed with sparse clarity – that he would even attempt such a work under such circumstances.

One can't possibly know, of course, how Bloch felt when he died. But he was very clear about the choices he made while he lived, in large measure because he spent the last years of his life explaining them. It is precisely his desire to explain what mattered to him, broadly defined, which made him an important writer. And it was his desire to do that explaining in terms of time, specifically defined, which made Bloch an important historian.

One can of course speak of many times in history (indeed, one of its great pleasures is a sense of time travel, of zooming back and forth across the past), but in the end I think there are only two: "now" and "not now." Depending on how you frame it, "now" might be the moment that began this morning, or when Christopher Columbus landed on Hispaniola in 1492, or when the last ice age ended. Conversely, "not now" might be that remote world on the far side of a dividing line marked by events like the birth of Christ, the Industrial Revolution, or Paris as it was before the Germans took over in the spring of 1940. Each of us thinks about what's "now" and "not now" differently and in multiple ways, depending on the context. Histories, in effect, are the strings of "now/not now" code we read and write to make sense of our lives.

But we don't simply passively accept what we understand to be "now" or "not now"; we also have a stance toward them. We may gladly consider a particular historical development (like, say, the emergence of the Internet) as marking the start of a time we call our own, and celebrate this "now." Conversely, we may be relieved that a particular period (Nazism, the age of the slave trade) can be safely considered "not now." Or we may lament the state of the world as we know it (one dominated by international finance capitalism) and seek to honor what we have lost through historical remembrance (by re-creating a time when labor unions were large and growing). Critics sometimes complain that that fixating on the past is mere nostalgia, useless longing for that which is irrecoverable – and not what we think it was in the first place. But good history is always more complex than that. It might be a matter of arguing that there are aspects of the past that are still alive – that what appears to be "not now" is really "now" after all. Or that there are pieces, always only pieces, of "not now" that can be resurrected into a *new* now one can imagine in the mind's eye – which is another way of saying the future. Because without some sense of what will be, even if it's nothing more than an imagined reader of words at a later date (perhaps only a not-now version of yourself), there can be no history.

But no historian records everything. Not even all the historians who have ever lived have collectively managed to do so. Life is too big, elusive, and ever-present for that. In the end, you have to choose what to talk about, and my final piece of advice to you is to choose what you love. (This is not to say you shouldn't choose to write about what you hate or fear, though that which you love should be at least implicit, if not spelled out.) Why did you choose that topic for that term paper? How might you connect what you've been *assigned* to talk about with what you *want* to talk about? And how might you tell somebody else what you care about in such a way that it helps them understand it (and help you understand yourself)? That someone else is crucial. In an important sense, writing is an ethical act: it means thinking about somebody other than you (and in history, it means thinking about the people who animate your sources, too). The wonderful paradox is that you come to understand yourself in learning about, and addressing, others. Make a habit of this, and you may not die a heroic death. But you're a lot more likely to have a wonderful, timeful life.

# Appendix A

# Writing an Essay: Ten Easy Steps in Review

So you have your topic, have gathered up some sources, and want to begin writing. (I mean after a doughnut or an episode of *The Daily Show*, when you're done procrastinating.) What now? Here's a suggested action plan derived from this book. If you get stuck, read/review chapters as necessary.

1. Dip into your sources. Read around. Look for surprising facts or other things that aren't obvious.
2. Decide: How do my sources affect my sense of the topic I've been asked or decide to explore? What do they prompt me to ask or change about what I've been thinking? ***This is your question.***
3. Formulate a one-sentence answer to the question. ***This is your thesis.***
4. Draft a paragraph that sets up your thesis with a relevant context, generalization, or observation, anchoring it toward the end. ***This is your intro.***
5. Break your thesis into component parts. Maybe a sequence of steps, for example. Or a bunch of *aspects* of the thesis.
6. Write a series of topic sentences on each of those steps/aspects. This will serve as an outline.
7. Fill in those topic sentences by explaining how and why they're true, giving facts, examples, and other kinds of evidence. ***This is your body.***

8.  Ask yourself: So what do I think now? Why does this all matter? (Think of an answer that involves the word "because"). Draft a one-sentence statement. *This is your motive.*
9.  Write a paragraph to situate and elaborate your motive by explaining its relationship with your thesis. *This is your conclusion.*
10. Go back and revise the introduction and body of the essay in light of what you've learned in the process of writing it. Up until now, you've been in *writerly* mode, trying to figure out what *you* think. Now go into *readerly* mode, trying to figure out what it will take for *someone else* to understand and accept what you think.

You think this is hard? You're damn right it is. And it never gets easy. But you will get better with practice, and the mere act of practice will improve the clarity not only of your writing, but also your reading and your thinking. That's always the goal.

Good luck and Godspeed.

153

# Appendix B
# Lending a Hand: Bibliographies and Footnotes

## 1. Why cite my sources?

Documenting your sources by citing them with footnotes and/or bibliographies is one of the most important practices of historical scholarship. And, by and large, students are terrible at it. I'm not really sure why. Part of me thinks it's because they're lazy; the mechanics are, after all, pretty simple, and if a student will just take the time to learn them, implementation is easy (very easy, in fact, with word processing programs, compared to the old days with typewriters). Another part of me thinks no, that's wrong; actually there are lots of ambiguities in citing, both in terms of where to do it and the format for less traditional sources like websites or movies. But in the end, it doesn't matter much why students are bad – the important thing (and it *is* an important thing) is that you get good.

Why? Narrowly speaking, because you're required to do so: Students who don't provide documentation of their sources risk punishment for plagiarism (see appendix C). But really, it's about being nice – and interesting. Serious readers of history periodically like to lift up the hood and see the engine in a piece of writing; they're always asking themselves: "Where did she get *that* nice little tidbit?" or "Whose line of interpretation is he following to build his case?" Writers who provide that kind of electronic paper trail tend to be appreciated. Those who don't not only lose points for clarity, but invite criticism on other grounds as well.

There are lots of different ways of documenting your sources, many of them discipline-specific. Literary discourse, for example, often uses the method developed by the Modern Language Association (MLA), which sometimes finds its way into history essays. There's nothing technically wrong with that, insofar as it gets the job done of showing where you got material by putting the author and page number in parentheses, augmented with a bibliography at the end (which students too often neglect to provide). But since history tends to use more sources than literary analysis, historical writing can get crowded with parentheses very quickly. That's why historians usually favor footnotes (at the bottom of a page) or endnotes (at the end of a document). You can recognize them by the little elevated numbers, known as superscript, that get slightly raised in the text, indicating that there will be more elaboration, whether in the form of bibliographic information or further explanation of a point that an author provides for readers who might be interested in more detail. The standard protocols for this kind of documentation is sometimes referred to as "Chicago" style, after the *Chicago Manual of Style*, which can be referenced most easily by referring to the most recent edition of Kate L. Turabian's *A Manual for Writers of Term Papers, Theses and Dissertations* (see appendix G for full citation).

## 2. When and where do I cite sources?

This is a source of great confusion for students. Some cite too much; others too little. The rule of thumb is this: Whenever you provide a fact or a quote that's not widely regarded as common knowledge, provide a footnote. Observing that July 4 is a national holiday in the United States does not require a footnote, nor does invoking the phrase "to be or not to be/that is the question." Noting that the Declaration of Independence was actually signed on July 2, not July 4, or quoting the phrase "cowards die many times before their deaths" does generally require a footnote. There is a gray area here; if your audience is historians of the American Revolution or Shakespeare plays (or, more specifically *Julius Caesar* scholars), such information is likely to be regarded as common knowledge, and so you might choose not to offer a footnote. Really the only way to be confident about this is to have experience with it, and the best way to gain experience is to read a lot of history – because, as this book has been at some pains to say, good reading and good writing are deeply intertwined. *When in doubt, err on the side of more, not less, documentation.*

The same holds true for where in the text you actually place a footnote. You have a bunch of options. One is immediately after you provide a fact or quote, even if it's right in the middle of a sentence. Generally speaking, that's not a good idea, because it breaks the flow of a reader's thinking. So unless your text is so chock full of data that you need to place a footnote there to avoid confusing a reader, avoid doing so. Most of the time, you can put the footnote at the end of a sentence. Sometimes, if you're using a bunch of facts from the same source, sprinkled over the course of a paragraph or even two paragraphs, you can wait and place the footnote at the end of the quote or paragraph(s). You can also place a footnote after the first of a series of sentences that rely on an important source, provide the information, and then follow it up by saying something like, "Much of the following information on topic X comes from Y's account," with Y being the footnoted source.

You also have the option of combining multiple sources into a single footnote. Let's say you have three pieces of data in a sentence. You can place a single footnote at the end of the sentence and then string together the information on each, in order, separated by semicolons (Smith 43; Jones 106). It should always be clear which citation refers to which fact, which you can clarify by adding a phrase like "on x, see (citation)"; "on y see (next citation)." In the event you think your reader will be confused, break things up as necessary to provide *clarity*. Because, whatever the particular rules, that's always the point.

### 3. How to I format a footnote?

After you've inserted a superscript number using your word processing software, you then need to provide the information a reader will need to track down the source herself. Generally speaking, that means author, title, place of publication, publisher, date of publication, and the relevant page numbers (if you're not referring to a book as a whole). For academic journals, include volume and number, along with the date in parentheses. There are variations and preferences for many of the cases that come up; you can never quite anticipate them all. But here are the general conventions for the kinds of sources you're more likely to use, based (though not entirely) on the *Chicago Manual of Style*.

**Preliminary note**: In the unlikely event that there's no page or date listed for a source, use "n.d." or "n.p."

**Also**: If you're using a remark quoted in a source, you can clarify in the footnote by saying, "Person X quoted in" and then give author, title, etc.

*Book*

1. Jim Cullen, *Born in the U.S.A.: Bruce Springsteen and the American Tradition* (New York: HarperCollins, 1997): 136.

If there's more than one author, list them as rendered on the title page.

*Journal article*

2. Jim Cullen, "Bruce Springsteen's Ambiguous Musical Politics in the Reagan Era," *Popular Music and Society* 16:2 (Summer 1992), 1–22.

Note that the "16" refers to the volume (typically counted annually), and the "2" refers to the number (typically correlating to a season). Thus there are usually four numbers for each volume – like 1 for spring, 2 for summer, 3 for fall, and 4 for winter. But vol. and no. can vary.

*Magazine article*

3. Jim Cullen, "The River: Crossroads of American History," *Backstreets*, Winter/Spring 2006, 29–31.

*Newspaper article*

4. Jim Cullen, "Analyzing the Republican Lexicon," *The Providence Journal-Bulletin,* October 28, 1991, A13.

*Encyclopedia article*

5. Jim Cullen, "The Popular Arts," in *The Encyclopedia of American Cultural and Intellectual History,* Vol. I., edited by Mary Kupiec Cayton and Peter W. Williams (New York: Charles Scribner's Sons, 2001), 647–656.

If there's no author listed for an encyclopedia article (or, for that matter, any other kind of article), simply begin with the title in quotation marks.

*Chapter or essay in an edited anthology*

6. Jim Cullen, "I's a Man Now: Gender and African American Men," in *Divided Houses: Gender and the Civil War,* edited by Catherine Clinton and Nina Silber (New York: Oxford University Press, 1992), 76–91.

*Book review*

7. Jim Cullen, review of *Memory's Nation: The Place of Plymouth Rock* by John Seelye, *The Journal of American History* 86:3 (December 1999): 1320.

*A book in second or multiple editions*

8. Jim Cullen, *Born in the U.S.A. Bruce Springsteen and the American Tradition* (1997; Middletown, CT: Wesleyan University Press, 2005).

Here the date of the first edition precedes the place of publication; you can also say "2nd ed." after the title instead, though I tend to prefer having the original date of publication, so that a reader can always know when a book was originally published.

*Article on a website*

9. Jim Cullen, "National Character: Daniel Day-Lewis, American Historian," *Common-Place*, July 2007, http://common-place.org/vol-07/no-04/school/ (give date accessed in parentheses).

Note: Because of the growing length and complexity of URLs, you may feel, as I do, that it makes more sense to give readers information they'll need to access easily via search engine rather than a string of type that may well be hard to reproduce accurately. So, for example, you may say something like:

10. Cullen quoted in Jon Pareles, "That's Dr. Boss to You: A Dropout as B.M.O.C.," *The New York Times*, October 28, 2000. Accessed via nytimes.com (give date).

*Website*

11. *American History for Cynical Beginners: Unrealistic Lessons for Everyday Life*, http://www.ecfs.org/projects/jcullen (give date).

*Non-print sources (sound and video)*

Though it is of course essential to note in the text when you when are drawing from them, and to include them in a bibliography, I don't regard footnoting non-print documents such as films and sound recordings as especially helpful, because unlike a book or website you can't easily scroll your way to a lyric or line of dialogue. It's also sometimes hard to sort out standard information like the producer of a film, because there may be many. But the basic facts you want to convey for a film are the title, producer, studio/production company, and date of original release. For a sound recording it's the artist, title, label, and release date. When it comes to particular songs or episodes from a film or TV series, you can make an analogy with print: As an article is to a book or magazine, so is a song to an album or an episode to a film. The song or episode goes in quotes, while the larger work gets italicized:

12. Kanye West, "Jesus Walks," *The College Dropout*, Roc-a-Fella records, 2004.
13. "How Titus Pullo Saved the Republic," *Rome*, HBO Home Video, 2007.

*References to the same text after the first citation*

You need not – should not – provide a full citation for a source more than once in footnotes or endnotes. If, later in an essay, you refer to a source again, you can generally abbreviate it using the author's name, followed by the page number:

14. Cullen, 191.

If you cite more than one source by the same author, you can abbreviate with the main title:

15. Cullen, *Born in the U.S.A.*, 132.
16. Cullen, "I's a Man Now," 81.

*Combining references*

You can batch more than one reference in a source, even if one source is being referred to for the first time, by using semi-colons:

17. Pareles, "That's Dr. Boss to You"; Jim Cullen, *Restless in the Promised Land: Catholics and the American Dream* (Franklin, Wisconsin: Sheed & Ward, 2001), 44.

## 4. How do I format a bibliography?

Bibliographies contain much of the same information footnotes do, but there are some important differences. The most important is that you use a bibliography to list *all* the sources you use in an essay, including background material, unlike a footnote, which refers to a specific source deployed in a specific place in an essay. Also, while you may refer to a source many times in your footnotes (albeit in abbreviated form after the first citation), a bibliography only lists a source once.

Some other key facts: bibliographies list sources alphabetically by the author's last name (unlike footnotes, where you put first names first). Bibliographies are also punctuated slightly differently, using periods after the name and title. Finally, bibliographies are formatted differently than footnotes or body text. Instead of indenting the first line of an entry, the first line in a bibliography is flush left, with the second and all subsequent lines indented.

*Book*

Cullen, Jim. *The American Dream: A Short History of an Idea that Shaped a Nation*. New York: Oxford University Press, 2003.

*Edited anthology*

Cullen, Jim, ed. *Popular Culture in American History*. Malden, MA: Blackwell, 2001.

If there's more than one author or editor for a book, use the surname, first name, for the first author and first name first for subsequent ones:

Sizer, Lyde C. and Jim Cullen, eds. *The Civil War Era: An Anthology of Sources*. Malden, MA: Blackwell, 2005.

*Chapter or essay in an edited anthology*

Cullen, Jim. "Fool's Paradise: Frank Sinatra and the American Dream." In *Popular Culture and American History*, edited by Jim Cullen. Malden, MA: Blackwell, 2001, 205–228.

*Newspaper/magazine article*

Cullen, Jim. "A Piece of the Dream." *Brown Alumni Monthly*, November/December 2002, 46–52.

For journal articles, give volume, number and date, just as you would with a footnote. For online journal articles, provide the search engine rather than a full URL:

Cullen, Jim. Review of *Race and Reunion: The Civil War in American Memory* by David Blight. *American Historical Review* 107:1 (February 2002). Accessed via JSTOR (give date).

*More than one source by the same author (alphabetize by title)*

Cullen, Jim. *The Art of Democracy: A Concise History of Popular Culture.* 1995; New York: Monthly Review Press, 2002.

——*Imperfect Presidents: Tales of Misadventure and Triumph.* New York: Palgrave, 2007.

——. "The White Picket Fence." Forbes.com, June 26, 2007. http://www.forbes.com/2007/06/26/american-dream-suburbs-biz-cx_de_dream0607_0626picket_land.html (give date of citation).

For other kinds of sources, use the sequence you find in footnotes (author, title, etc.) and the punctuation of bibliographies (periods, no parenthesis for publisher/date), etc.


## 5. A final note

The formats for most of the other kinds of sources you're likely to cite can be extrapolated from the footnote/bibliography examples noted above (you can of course also consult another reference source or ask your teacher). In the event of any doubt, invoke the golden rule by asking yourself: "If I was the reader of this footnote or bibliography entry, what would I need to be able to track it down?" Even if your technical proficiency is imperfect, the spirit of your thought and intention counts.

# Appendix C

# Credit Scams:
# The Dangers of Plagiarism

Plagiarism – the offense of passing off other people's ideas or words as one's own – is a touchy subject. For a few students, it's an alluring, shadowy temptation. For a few more, it's a source of anxiety generating fears of accidental crime and unforeseen retribution. For most teachers, it's a serious matter they're vigilant about, even as they know it's likely some infractions sneak under the radar. I will confess that I myself sometimes think too much is made of plagiarism, in part because the issue has been exploited by publishing executives and lawyers who take an excessively proprietary view of what they're fond of calling intellectual property.

But neither my view of the matter nor yours is particularly relevant. The fact is that you live in a time and place where plagiarism is considered a serious matter, and you have an obligation, if for no other reason than the security of your academic and subsequent career prospects, to know what it is and not to do it. A key part of that is avoiding situations where it might seem like a feasible option. Most of the plagiarists I've known have said they made the choice out of desperation – time was short and they were looking for a quick fix. So I'll say once more with feeling: Writing takes time. Give yourself enough to do it, and you'll avoid a whole lot of problems, among them the temptation to plagiarize.

Plagiarism can take many forms. The most obvious, and annoying, is when you cite statistics or little-known facts without saying where they came from, either in a phrase like "According to X in her book Y," or a footnote (you should have both). You can't simply say, "British expenditures in the thirteen colonies between 1754 and 1763 may have totaled three million pounds, a sum almost half the size of one of the Crown's prewar budgets." You *must* say where you got this information. In this particular case, it's Kevin Phillips, *Wealth and Democracy: A Political History of the American Rich* (New York: Broadway Books, 10). When I look at *Phillips's* sources, I see *he* got the data for the paragraph from which this sentence is quoted in Edwin Burroughs's and Mike Wallace's *Gotham: A History of New York City to 1898* (New York: Oxford University Press, 1998, 168–70), though I must say he's a bit murky about it, because his method of citation, which relies on page numbers rather than footnotes or endnotes, is imprecise. Ideally, you'll track down *Gotham* and use *it* as the source of your data. But that's not always possible. The point, in any case, is to leave tracks behind for anyone who wants to follow them back.

Another obvious form of plagiarism is when you copy, or merely slightly rearrange, someone else's words and fail to give them credit. Here's the opening of the first chapter in John Demos's vivid and gripping *The Unredeemed Captive: A Family Story from Early America* (1994; New York: Vintage, 1995):

> Deerfield, Massachusetts. October 1703. Harvest over. First frost. The valley ablaze in color: reds and yellows at the sides (along with the forested green ridges of East Mountain and the lower hills to the west), green of the meadows in between. The river low and languorous, a glassy rope snaked through the center. The most beautiful month, sunset of the year.
>
> Do the townspeople notice? No, they are fixed on the night ahead. Danger grows in the darkening corners. *Night of winter, night of want, night of war.*

It's not enough to avoid trouble simply by rearranging words. "October 1703. Deerfield, Massachusetts. First frost; the harvest over" – that's plagiarism. Even a whole set of other words that conjure up a gorgeous New England landscape and then cut suddenly to a terrified village fearing an Indian raid would be problematic. If you're not stealing the content, you're stealing the spirit of Demos's talent and vision. Give the man credit.

Other forms of plagiarism may seem less obvious to you. Let's say, for example, you look through a dozen sources for a research paper you're writing, but find that only four of them are actually quoted in the essay you write. And let's say you footnote those four sources scrupulously. You might still be guilty of plagiarism if you fail to note that some of the remaining eight really did affect your thinking (like, say, the time frame you chose for the essay). One way of avoiding the problem is to follow up on a source you do cite by saying something like, "My thinking about this subject was also influenced by Y's discussion of it in ..." and add that citation to the footnote. Another is include the source in a bibliography that accompanies the footnotes. Many scholars annotate their bibliographies with brief descriptions of their sources (see, for example, Katie Martell's bibliography in chapter 15), or include bibliographic essays that are sometimes less precise but more reader-friendly. These, too, are options for you.

Still another murky situation occurs when you look at a friend's essay, or have a long discussion with another teacher, or have a parent or tutor edit your drafts. None of these practices are against the law, of course, and in many cases are actually a good idea. But noting the range and depth of such help is an ethical requirement. Many teachers and schools have taken to having their students write brief acknowledgments with their essays along the lines you often see in books. Something like, "The author would like to his dad, Bill, for background information on Polish immigration"; or "I'm grateful for the help of my tutor, Erin Rodriguez, for helping make, and structure, a distinction between X and Y in my essay."

As with so many other things in life, intentions count: If you don't *want* to plagiarize, you probably won't. Of course, intentions aren't everything. Much of closing the rest of the gap between intention and action is forethought. Ask yourself: Are my attributions clear here? Is the teacher going to know that this is me talking?

It's also important to add here that there are many kinds of information that really don't need attribution. Saying that George Washington was the first president of the United States is pretty much common knowledge. Actually, citing the more obscure fact that James Madison was the fourth president of the United States is still pretty much common information. You don't really need to attribute the phrase "all men are created equal" to Thomas Jefferson. Saying "the earth belongs to the living," by contrast, might require a footnote – unless your audience is a Jefferson scholar in a Jefferson class where many of his famous lines have been long discussed. Context counts. Here as in so many ways, *thinking* – a practice that can somehow get lost amid the pressure of deadlines and trying to fit the process into a formula – is the key.

There may be some readers among you who are asking themselves, "But why, really, shouldn't one cut such corners?" Undeniably, doing so can make the often painful process of writing go more smoothly and easily. Undeniably, too, plagiarism escapes detection, maybe even most of the time. No less a great figure than Martin Luther King, Jr. was a plagiarist.[1] Besides, people in other eras never worried about things like copyrights – Shakespeare never footnoted his plays or worried about stealing plots for his drama.

I could reply by noting that plagiarism is against the law, and while it's relatively unlikely you would ever be sued or convicted of the crime, stranger things have happened (along with more common ones like getting suspended or expelled from your school). But I'll focus my response, and end this discussion, with a modified form of a handout I've been known to circulate at my school.

## Five reasons not to cheat on an essay assignment

1. Teachers are not always as dumb as they look (especially when grading the work of students who are not as smart as they think).

[1] King's plagiarism is now considered common knowledge among scholars of his life and work. For an acknowledgment from a reputable source, and some of the issues involved, see the article discussing the matter on Stanford University's Martin Luther King, Jr.'s Research and Education Institute website: http://www.stanford.edu/group/King/additional_resources/articles/palimp.htm (accessed July 23, 2007).

2. Cheating well takes time and effort – particularly as teachers and administrators grow more savvy in mapping out unsavory paper mill websites and subscribe to sophisticated software designed to catch plagiarists.

3. Even when it succeeds, cheating generates suspicions that may or may not be apparent to the cheater.

4. Letter of recommendation, anyone? (Please?) Damaged credibility is hard to repair.

5. Cheating is wrong, and hard as it may be to believe, some people actually take ethical matters seriously.

# Appendix D
# Web of Lies?
# Weighing the Internet

*Note: For more information on the possibilities and limits of the Internet, see chapter 5.*

It sometimes seems that if students had their choice, *every* essay they wrote would draw on sources drawn solely from the World Wide Web. And that if teachers had their choice, *no* essay students wrote would use online sources. This is, of course, an oversimplification. Most students realize there are any number of valuable sources that are not available online, and all scholars know that the volume of quality material available on the Internet is growing exponentially. But they also know that the volume of junk sources is growing exponentially, too. Your job in writing an essay is not simply a matter of choosing good sources, but developing a sense of judgment about online resources you feel comfortable with and return to again and again, and how to evaluate a new online source and vouch for its credibility. The following are some questions you can ask yourself as you surf in scholarly mode.

## What's the domain?

Though it was founded by the U.S. government (specifically the Defense Department) and academic institutions, and for a long time resisted overtly commercial uses, many of us now think of the Internet as a predominately commercial enterprise – dot.com seems to be the most common suffix for Universal Resource Locators (URLs). Certainly, there are any number of for-profit web resources that are highly credible sources of information; nytimes.com comes to mind, as do a number of other print- and broadcast-based websites with strong archival resources. But websites that exist primarily for the sake of commerce – beware of pages that are littered with advertisements for seemingly random products – should be used with care, if at all. Government sources (ending in .gov) can often be considered excellent sources of statistics, particularly census figures. But they should not be taken at face value when dealing with controversial subjects, or when the government in question is known to be unstable or corrupt. Non-governmental organizations, or NGOs (.org) often have expertise in specific areas and can provide a perspective official sources do not. But, perhaps not surprisingly, academic sites (those ending .edu) are among the safest for use in an academic essay.

That's not to say you shouldn't do some shopping around. Often you'll find that a primary source like the letters of a famous person can be found at more than one university website. Some are definitely better than others in terms of how complete their documentation is and the quality of the commentary. So *always* look at a few versions of a document when you have the option, and decide what you consider the most complete, reliable, and user-friendly repository of the information in question.

## Who's the publisher?

One of the great things about the Web is its profoundly democratic character: Anyone can launch a website, declare themselves an expert, and say pretty much whatever he pleases. That's fine in any number of contexts, but when it comes to historical sources, you want to be able to vet the people or organization. Blogs littered with lots of first-person opinions should be regarded skeptically, as should sites that appear to promote or encourage strong views without evidence to back them up. Any reputable person or institution will have some kind of "about us" sketch on or easily accessible to the home page, giving the visitor an easy opportunity to weigh credentials and assess credibility.

## Free or subscription?

As you know first-hand, there's all kinds of great stuff out there that's merely a click away. This includes first-class portals like *History Cooperative*, which collects articles from a stable of the most prestigious scholarly journals of history, as well as more general ones like Google Scholar, which may yet absorb and/or render all challengers obsolete. But the very best historical portals tend to be those that are maintained on a subscription basis, typically sold to libraries and accessible to you as an account holder at your school. Some, like *Social Sciences Index* (also called *Social Sciences Full Text*), *JSTOR*, or *America, History and Life* have huge databases of academic journals that you often have to limit with advanced searches to produce manageable results from a search. Others, like *Rotunda* (which specializes in primary source documents in early U.S. history), are more boutique databases with elegant interfaces and rich documentation. Such databases are coming, going, and being combined all the time, which is one reason why I'm not listing the URLs here (a quick google is all it will take). It's also why a conversation with a librarian early in your research – and thus a trip to the library – makes a lot of sense.

## Is it updated?

Already in its short life, the Web has become littered with defunct or little-maintained sites whose data becomes dated even more decisively than some print sources. That doesn't necessarily mean that information from old sites is useless, but that it should be used with care. You might want to follow up on anything intriguing that you find to see if new information has surfaced about it in the time since the data was posted. The Internet not only has a history, it *is* history, and one that will only become longer and richer as the twenty-first century proceeds.

# Appendix E
# DBQs and Reviews

As you know, most of the focus in this book has been on writing essays – a term I intentionally left a little vague because I mean for it to encompass a variety of writing assignments that run the gamut from a brief reaction to a night's reading to a semester-long term paper. But there are specific varieties of essays that may come up fairly often in your history career, so I thought I'd say a few words about two of the most important ones (for discussion of another, comparison/contrast essays, see chapter 11).

## Document-Based Questions (DBQs)

Most commonly associated with the Advanced Placement (AP) exam many students take in high school, DBQs are a useful pedagogical tool utilized in other kinds of exams as well (many teachers like myself also use old DBQs as a staple of our classroom teaching). What's nice about them is that they're like microwave dinners: the meal is to a great extent prepared in advance. You have the ingredients in the form of sources edited into small servings. In terms of argument (see chapter 8), you also have the question, which is given to you at the outset. Because of time pressures, motives tend not to be important. So the real focus of a DBQ is the thesis. Put most of your mental energy there.

Given that there are often time pressures involved in taking such exams, it's worth reminding you of two obvious things that may be easy to lose sight of as you plunge into responding:

1. Read the question carefully.
2. Read *all* the documents. They're there for a reason.

Did I remind you to read the question? Be sure to read the question. Read the question at the beginning, at the middle, and, *especially* when you think you're done – very often you'll stray from the point without even realizing it. Can't overstate the point: **Read that question.**

It's important here to make a distinction between a DBQ *topic* and a DBQ *question*. Very often, the former will (perhaps misleadingly) take the form of a yes or no question: "Did Germany have a Revolution?" "Was the Progressive Movement Radical?" But the actual question is almost always more nuanced statement: "*Evaluate the extent to which* Germany underwent a revolutionary transformation." As you head into the essay, be sure to stay focused on the actual question. Almost never will you give a straight-up yes or no answer. Don't be wishy-washy; take a real stand. But that stand should be relative rather than absolute, and be aware of possible counterarguments. Something like, "Yes, Germany did undergo a revolution, in the sense that its political institutions changed, even if no shots were actually fired." Or: "No, Germany did not undergo a bona fide revolution, even though significant political changes did occur."

It may well be helpful to attend to your gut even before you look at the documents in any detail (at least a preliminary glance may well be necessary, though). Remember, you're making an *argument* here. You're going to need to have an opinion and to defend it. That's not to say you shouldn't read the documents carefully, and you should definitely be willing to change your mind. But having some sort of starting point, even if you yourself know it's wobbly, can help you sort out your thinking.

Once you're clear on the question and your preliminary response, zero in on defining key terms. What do you understand the word "revolution" or "radical" (or, for that matter, "Progressive" or even "Germany") to mean? Do the documents give you any clues? Do any of those documents run counter to your instinctive sense of what those words are? Try to sort that out, because until you have a sense of how you're going to define your terms, the thesis is not going to come into focus.

When it does (or starts to, anyway), begin outlining. Pick the documents you think will best help you make your case. Highlight the passages you think you want to quote. Identify those that challenge your view and think about how you might respond to them. Then make an outline, perhaps in the form of topic sentence-like phrases.

When you actually begin to use the document, remember to *show*, not *tell*. Don't write things like "as Document H says," without actually identifying the passage you mean. Also, remember, your job is not to report but *analyze* (see chapter 7 for more on this). *Use* the information; *interpret* it. That may mean editing quotes and jumping from one to another, which is fine, as long as you're clear about it and always identify the speaker.

When you're subject to time pressure, it's generally not possible to polish your work, and that generally means that the motive part of an argument gets short shrift. But if you have the time and insight, try to develop the implications of your thesis a bit as you revise (see chapter 8). Be particularly attentive to the frame as you revise (see chapter 14).

Finally: Keep track of time. You'll need to decide on a provisional thesis within a few minutes of getting the question. Try to pace yourself and leave time for looking over your work.

*Special thanks to Andy Meyers of the Fieldston School History Dept., whose guide to taking the DBQ, available at his website (http://www.ecfs. org/projects/fieldston57/) was of invaluable assistance.*

## Book (or other) reviews

Reviewing is a staple practice of the writing profession. When a teacher asks you to write a review, she's usually trying to develop two skills: Your ability to describe what a document is saying on the document's terms (the argument, and how it's put together), and your ability to assess that document on *your* terms. This can sometimes get tricky if the document in question has multiple perspectives, as in a novel or documentary, because there are a series of people whose views need to be taken into account: the characters or subjects who express views in the document; its author or authors (whose views may or may not be the same as those of those who speak in the document); and yourself. It's vitally important as you proceed that you know at any given moment whose point of view you're conveying to your reader. Perhaps ironically, this can get tricky when you agree with much of what's being said, because you may confuse your reader (or even yourself) about whose views are being expressed at any given time, and/or the *basis* of agreement – in what *sense* is person X right? Phrases like "person X is right in the sense that" or "while I don't necessarily agree with person X on matter Y, I do think she's right about Z," might help.

As someone who's written a few reviews in his life, I've developed a formula I use when writing them. I'm not slavishly devoted to it, and it might not work at all or in part for you. But in the event it will help, here it is:

1. **Establish a context.** Begin a review with a relevant generalization. Note that the topic of the document you're reviewing is one that has beguiled, bedeviled, or bemused observers in one way or another for some time or another. Be as specific as possible – ideally by identifying famous people or works associated with the subject. Situate the document you're reviewing in this context toward the end of the introduction, and tilt your hand as to how you feel about it – what you think is new in its handling of its subject, whether you like it, and a sense of why. *This will be **your** argument about the **document's** argument.*

2. **Describe what the book is about.** Explain what the author's thesis is, how the book is structured, and the aspects of the subject he deems most important. (Here you may also talk about various characters or scenarios and how they reflect or shape the larger point of view of the document.) The key is to describe the text on the *author's* terms, not yours, to convey a sense of fairness.

**3. Describe what the book is *really about* – in effect, its *motive*** (see chapter 8). Why does what the author says matter? How does this document fit into the big picture you talk about in your introduction? *In effect, the document's **motive** becomes your **thesis***. (See chapter 8 for more on this.)

**4. Now it's time to move to evaluation,** to state explicitly what you think of the document. You may well have conveyed this subtly through various choices you've made to this point (like your diction). But now it's time to explain and justify your opinion. *In effect, your opinion of what the author is doing becomes your motive.*

**5. Circle back to the original context.** Where do we go from here? What might a better book have done to address the issues? How does this book's excellence answer some questions – and perhaps raise others?

Simmer as necessary. Cool with time to revise, and serve.

# Appendix F
# A Glossary of Key Terms

The following is a list of important words and phrases used in this book that describe the construction and uses of an academic essay. Words in italics (except for "essay" itself) are defined elsewhere in this glossary. The chapter or chapters where further discussion of these terms can be found is listed in brackets.

*Analysis.* The act of breaking down a text or subject into its component parts for evaluation. Analysis represents value added by the person performing it; it goes beyond what a text or person is explicitly saying to suggest something that's not obvious or unsaid. [8]

*Argument.* A line of reasoning designed to convince a thoughtful skeptic. The argument of an essay consists of a *question*, a *thesis*, and a *motive*. It is typically unveiled in the *introduction*, and sustained throughout an essay as a whole. [8]

*Audience.* The reader a writer imagines for an essay. Even in those cases where a writer knows the specific person or persons who will be reading his essay, he will still have to try to anticipate questions and responses to things he's never said before in quite the same way. The greater the clarity a writer has about his audience, the more readable an essay will seem. [8]

*Body.* The middle, or trunk, of an essay. The body usually consists of a series of paragraphs governed *by topic sentences*. It is the main repository of *evidence*, and the place where *counterevidence* and *counterargument* are often considered. The *introduction* and *conclusion*, which bound it on either side, are places an *argument* gets defined or elaborated; the body is where it that argument justified and explained. [10–12]

**Conclusion**. The final paragraph or paragraphs of an essay. Often a site of recapitulation or summary, the conclusion is also where the *motive* typically comes into focus. The conclusion, along with the *introduction*, form the *frame* of an essay, which define its *argument*. [13]

**Counterargument**. An alternative or contradictory line of reasoning to that which a writer is advancing in the *argument* in an essay. Good writers will acknowledge, and somehow come to terms with, counterarguments. [12]

**Counterevidence**. Facts, quotes, or other data that appear to, or actually do, contradict other such data being used in an *argument* in an essay. Good writers will acknowledge, and somehow come to terms with, counterevidence. [12]

**Diction**. The series of word choices a writer uses in the process of construction of an essay. Diction is often crucial to the success of an *argument*, both in terms of providing concise terminology as well as conveying a point of view. It is particularly important in the realm of *motive*, as the right verb or adjective can convey a writer's attitude or feeling about the subject in question. [9, 14]

**Double signposts**. A form of *stitching* in which words or phrases ("in addition"; "another example"; "nevertheless") are used, often in topic sentences or at the end of paragraphs, that link what came immediately before in a discussion to what will follow. [12]

**Evidence**. Information, facts, quotations, or other data used to support a *thesis*. *Arguments* can be articulated without evidence, but evidence is essential for them to be persuasive. Evidence is typically housed in the *body* of an essay. [12]

**Essay**. As a noun: a relatively short piece of expository writing designed to convey an author's point of view about a subject. As a verb: to attempt, or try, as in a line of thinking to be considered by the writer in the act of composition and a reader in the act of reading. [Introduction]

**Exposition**. Prose that sets up, explains, and connects the various pieces on an essay, particularly *evidence*. Exposition typically appears in the sentences that follow the *topic sentence* in a paragraph. Its natural home is in the body of an essay. [11]

**Frame/Framing**. The frame refers to the *introduction* and *conclusion* of an essay as a unit, a conceptualization often useful in the revision stage for the fullest articulation and focus of the *argument*. Framing is a practice of tightening the relationship between the *introduction, conclusion,* and *topic sentences* during revision. [14]

**Historiography**. While the term can be used to refer to any kind of historical document, historiography typically refers to the history of History as a discipline, or the specific discourse on a particular subject as it has unfolded over time. [2]

**Inter-paragraph organization**. The degree of coherence in an essay, particularly in the *body*, as defined by the logical flow of *topic sentences*. If a reader can read the first sentence of a string of paragraphs in sequence and feel that the essay as a whole can be followed coherently, that essay can be said to have good inter-paragraph organization. [10]

**Intra-paragraph organization**. The degree of coherence within a paragraph, particularly in the flow of sentences that follow the *topic sentence*. If a reader feels like a series of paragraphs are internally coherent, they can be said to have good intra-paragraph organization. [10]

**Introduction**. The opening paragraph (or, occasionally, paragraphs) of an essay. The introduction (or "intro" for short) typically consists of context, relevant generalization, and, especially, the *argument*. Intros are crucial to the success of an essay, and often require the most active work in conceptualization and revision. The introduction and *conclusion* form the *frame* of an essay, which fully define its *argument*. [9]

**Key term**. Word or concept crucial to explaining or justifying an *argument*. Key terms, which typically appear in or near the *introduction*, must be defined for the purposes of discussion in an essay. [9]

**Motive**. An implication or extrapolation the follows from the *thesis* of an essay. Often broached in the *introduction*, it usually gets its fullest elaboration in the *conclusion* of an essay. [8]

**Premise**. A proposition or idea that forms the basis of a *thesis*. If a thesis is a statement that is *not* obvious but true, a premise is a statement that is both obvious and true, but which needs to be articulated in order for a thesis to be understood or accepted. A premise is typically stated in the *introduction*. [9]

**Primary source.** A first-hand account of the past typically recorded by someone who participated or witnessed the event in question, or (like a journalist) narrated events soon afterward. Primary sources are distinguished from *secondary sources*, which are documents made by third parties long after the fact. [3]

**Question.** A concisely formulated inquiry designed to advance understanding of a subject. In the specific context of an essay, a question is a core component of an *argument* and becomes the basis of a *thesis*. [4, 8]

**Readerly mode.** Phase of the writing process in which a writer, having articulated her *argument* to her own satisfaction, now thinks in terms of clarity and persuasiveness for an *audience* beyond herself. [14]

**Rhythm.** The sense of pace or flow in an essay. Often defined by variation in sentence length. Too many short sentences results in choppiness; too many long ones get hard to follow. Prose with good rhythm is pleasingly varied. It typically gets improved in the revision process. [14]

**Secondary source.** An account of the past typically recorded some time after the fact, typically by someone who was not present at the event in question. Secondary sources contrast with *primary sources*, which record an event as or immediately after it occurs. [3]

**Source/Sources.** The basic building block of history, its indispensable ingredient. All stories about the past draw on someone else's account of events (otherwise they're memoir, fiction, or some other genre of writing). Such accounts typically take two forms: *primary sources* and *secondary sources*. [3]

**Stitching.** Any number of devices (repeated words or phrases, *double signposts*, parallel structures in *topic sentences*, or other strategies) that serve to hold the pieces of an essay together. Stitching sometimes emerges organically in an essay, but can also be added as part of the revision process. [14]

**Thesis.** A not-obvious, but true assertion that forms the core of an *argument*. In an essay, a *thesis* responds to a question and prompts a *motive*. [8]

**Topic sentence.** A statement, typically at the start of a paragraph, which governs that paragraph as a whole, either by defining a subject or explaining what comes next. More so than in other kinds of prose, topic sentences play a crucial role in essays, and often define their contours. [10]

***Writerly mode.*** Phase of the drafting process where the writer of an essay thinks chiefly in terms of sketching out an *argument* and structure with little concern for clarity or persuasiveness beyond the writer herself. Thinking in writerly mode is often essential in the earliest stages and to prevent paralyzing concerns about what a reader will think. [14]

# Appendix G
# More Reading About Writing

The following bibliography lists some of the works on writing and/ or historiography that I consulted in the process of writing this book. Much of the information and advice in them is identical to that which you will find here (such as how to format a footnote), and yet each has its own emphasis and strengths (I pay special attention to the challenges of writing in an essay format, for example). Generally speaking, I list the most recent edition available, even if I happened to use an earlier one, because newer ones are likely to be more easily available, if not better. Of course, by the time you encounter this list, some of these books may well have been reissued again. Titles with an asterisk are ones whose tone, content, and availability are among those I believe are most likely to help students grappling with the issues discussed in this book.

Arnold, John H. *History: A Very Short Introduction*. New York: Oxford University Press, 2000.

Bloch. Marc. *The Historian's Craft*, trans. by Peter Putnam. New York: Vintage, 1954.

*Booth, Wayne C., Gregory G. Colombo, and Joseph M. Williams. *The Craft of Research*, 2nd edn. Chicago: University of Chicago Press, 2003.

*Brundage, Anthony. *Going to the Sources: A Guide to Historical Writing*, 4th edn. Wheeling, IL: Harlan Davidson, 2008.

Carr, E. H. *What is History?* New York: Knopf, 1961.

Gilderhus, Mark T. *History and Historians: A Historiographical Introduction*, 6th edn. Upper Saddle River, NJ: Pearson Prentice-Hall, 2007.

*Harvey, Gordon. *Writing with Sources: A Guide for Students*. Indianapolis: Hackett Publishing Company, 1998.

Howell, Martha and Walter Prevenier. *From Reliable Sources: An Introduction to Historical Methods*. Ithaca, NY: Cornell University Press, 2001.

Lunsford, Angela and John J. Ruszkiewicz. *Everything's an Argument*, 4th edn. Boston: Bedford/St. Martin's 2006.

Marius, Richard. *A Short Guide to Writing About History*, 6th edn. New York: Longman, 2006.

Novick, Peter. *That Noble Dream: The "Objectivity Question" and the American Historical Profession*. Cambridge, UK: Cambridge University Press, 1988.

*Rampolla, Mary Lynn. *A Pocket Guide to Writing about History*, 5th edn. Boston: Bedford/St. Martin's, 2006.

Ross, Dorothy. *The Origins of American Social Science*. Cambridge, UK: Cambridge University Press, 1991.

*Storey, William Kelleher. *Writing History: A Guide for Students*, 2nd edn. New York: Oxford University Press, 2004.

Strunk William Jr. and E. B. White. *The Elements of Style*, 4th edn. Boston: Allyn & Bacon 1999.

Turabian, Kate L. *A Manual for Writers of Term Papers, Theses and Dissertations*, 6th edn. Chicago: University of Chicago Press, 1996.

Williams, David R. *Sin Boldly! Dr. Dave's Guide to Writing the College Paper*. Cambridge, MA: Perseus Publishing, 2000.

Wilson, Norman J. *History in Crisis? Recent Directions in Historiography*, 2nd edn. Upper Saddle, NJ: Pearson Prentice-Hall, 2005.

# Index

*Index*

186